Amazing Mentors

The REAL Hot Mamas Path to Power

Compiled by Karilee Halo Shames PhD, RN

Amazing Mentors

The REAL Hot Mamas
Path to Power

Compiled by Karilee Halo Shames PhD, RN

ISBN: 978-1-939625-15-1
Library of Congress Control Number: 2013900643

Published by Inkwell Productions
10869 N. Scottsdale Road # 103-128
Scottsdale, AZ 85254-5280

Tel. 480-315-3781
E-mail info@inkwellproductions.com
Website www.inkwellproductions.com

Printed in the United States of America

Dedication

Many powerful women helped pave my way.
I stand on the shoulders of great and tiny
women of all colors, shapes, and sizes;
It's a great view here.

I dedicate this book to my strong and amazing mother, Gloria Deutsch Hirsch, who gave me life and her strength.

With fond memories of my grandmothers, Fanny Guterman Feibus and Mae Kelmenson Deutsch…

Love to our daughters Shauna-Lani, and Dr. Gigi, and to our son, Gabriel Benjamin. My eternal appreciation goes to kindly caring wonderful Rich, Cousin Sherry, and Lynn Larkin.

Special thanks go to Shauna Shames, and to Suzanna Gratz of Inspiring Promotions, for their expert editorial support.

I stand in awe of the process…when women birth our dreams…together.

Contents

Muses in Our Midst

As our first daughter approached puberty, I suggested she invite a circle of women from our dance class to share their wisdom with her.

The women came, and began to share their secrets. One by one, these magnificent women told stories of their lives. When the last story was told, our hearts were open and our circle was complete.

Then, surprisingly, the woman who first shared wanted to share again. These real Hot Mamas, one by one, shared again, each at a deeper level. By the third time around, we were bonded for life. It was a spontaneous, sacred and blessed event.

Some of these women had never shared their stories aloud. Stories of first love never forgotten. And of first love remembered, in vivid detail. Of rose petals, strewn on lovely beds, with candles to brighten the dark. Stories of hearts broken open and pain we could never have imagined.

Both the telling and receiving of each story wove a magical tapestry of sisterhood.

Here, I share powerful stories of women who helped me learn to grow. They are great and everyday women, willing to evolve, sharing their stories with joys and warts. They are REAL women willing to learn from life; to help you better understand.

I want all women to know how lovely and special we are. To spend less time worrying about details that won't matter. And more time on what matters to you.

I want you to evolve yourselves . . .
Younger women, into the beautiful blossom that only **you** can be. Older women, to shed any fears, fully living with what may be left undone.

May this book inspire you to reach out and learn from life, enjoying it all, so you can inspire the women around you.

If it does, please pass it forward to your daughters, granddaughters, and to their daughters, so women can be all that we are.

Follow the powerful path of your "mamas" so you can live your most abundant life.

captive. She told me she would punch in my breasts. That was the memory that stuck. It took me decades to stop hating my breasts.

It was a tough time for all of us. Around those years, our family moved, we kids started new schools, and our parents were under terrible financial pressures. This level of stress surely contributed to my mother's emotional meltdowns.

I was a highly sensitive, highly emotional teenager, prone to my own hormonal meltdowns with my volatile mother, who broke her arm in one of our embattled encounters when I was just fifteen years old. Fortunately, my angels protected me and amazingly, I suffered no injuries of my own. I didn't know whether to laugh or cry over my good fortune, but it was embarrassing for the six weeks my mother wore that cast. I knew even then that it wasn't at all about whatever subject set off her screaming fits. It was the raw unadulterated rage which she didn't have the skill to contain.

Thankfully, my mom has grown into a dear and enjoyable friend. I have come to accept that she did the best she could. Now I can better see that she was on her own schedule, healing from the wounds of her life, wounds that ran deep.

Back then, in my final high school year, a crisis precipitated a major step for me. Months before my graduation, we lost our beautiful home. At that time, our family moved into my grandmother's house. I realized that to go to college, I would need a scholarship. I worked hard to excel, graduating in the top five percent of my high school graduating class and cum laude in college. It was hard to be special at large schools, but I gave it my all.

I knew that nursing was my calling. It was intertwined with my personal search for healing and a deeper meaning. As a teen, I had been a weekend volunteer candy striper in our nearby hospital. My first real job was in high school, as assistant at a nursing home. Near graduation, I began to apply for any scholarship I could attain. By August, I was in a state of panic when I finally received the letter: I was one of 100 students from across the US to be accepted into the Walter Reed Army Institute of Nursing (WRAIN) Program. My first two years would be spent at the University of Maryland, a huge school. After completing the required courses there, I transferred to Walter Reed.

I was a member of the US Army from 1967-1970, during the Vietnam War. Yes, I am a veteran. My patients, forty soldiers to a ward, were missing arms, legs, stomachs, and faces. Some were diagnosed with unspeakable cancers. Very often, mental problems from PTSD compounded their many health issues. Day after day, all I could think was "these men could be my brothers."

Linda Seely; Me; Kerry Gardner; and Ellen Heuer at the old nurses dorm,
Walter Reed Army Medical Center (1969-1970)

Healing: Becoming Whole

As a young woman, I thought finding a man would fulfill me.
Later, even when happily married, insecurities lingered. Our
children, with their nonstop loving and noisy demands, filled the
hole in my heart for years, but then they grew, up and away and
I knew I still needed to complete my healing.

Looking back, it makes sense that I went into nursing. Likewise,
it makes sense that I now volunteer for abused women and
children. And in addition to leading a weekly therapy group at
the nearby "Women's Safe House," I've been accompanying
women to Domestic Violence court, helping them get through

the process of securing restraining orders against their batterers. I have also taught about domestic violence in our local schools, all part of my own healing journey.

Life has eventually shown me how whole I am – but only after I learned to reclaim my broken parts. I learned that healing is a process of reclaiming everything that happened in our lives: the good, bad and the ugly, and learning to transform and bless it all. And then we move on.

I spent my twenties disentangling from the tribe of my birth, seeking wisdom from well-chosen mentors, modeling joyful lives. By far, the best path was in following Napoleon Hill's advice, creating a "Mastermind" circle of fabulous (female) advisors.

Capturing the essence of these women, learning to bring their wisdom into my life, enabled me to grow in ways I never could have dreamed. Along the way I was "adopted" by certain teachers, who saw something in me. They inspired me to be my best, to move forward; and to shine my light.

A lovely psychiatric nursing instructor named Darlene Hall believed in me, encouraging me to seek a MS degree in psych nursing. With her help I received National Institute of Mental Health grant. At the master's level, I had great instructors who nourished and inspired me, including Dr. Lisa Robinson and Dr. Delores McManama at University of Maryland.

At Walter Reed, an Army Major was our medical-surgical instructor. She is featured in this book forty years later! There, she helped us as young women to overcome our fears, caring for wounded soldiers, forty to a ward. Later she became a General in the US Army, one of the very few women to ever achieve such success. Today, decades later, she remains an inspiration to me; and to those who know her. Thanks to her way of teaching, we learned to make a difference.

I co-founded an organization, in 1977, called Nurses In Transition with a nurse named Dianne Duchesne. It started in San Francisco, but eventually groups also formed in Boston, New York, and a number of other locations. My goal was to bring nurses together, to help them move from a hospital-based practice to one that had more of a sense of independence. The work inspired many nurses and was the beginning of a new direction for my profession.

The editor in her early years
of nursing

I learned that healing comes from a root word "halos, or haelen" to become whole and hearty, which was what I had sought my entire life. I discovered that by surrounding myself with great women, I could grow and heal from my own wounds. I feel blessed to have been given a dream, and the strength to have found ways to live it. I've learned from my female mentors how to communicate more effectively, how to speak my heart and to not offend; how to be assertive and not aggressive. I've realized that gifts are given to us. Then, as we mature, we must give them back. I found that I loved inspiring nurses, and other women – as we are all engaged in healing.

Letting the Real Hot Mamas Guide You

Today, my need to pass this wisdom on is as great a need as was my need to learn it. I am pleased to be able to mentor others, including young girls and their mothers, as well as all women, so they can enjoy better, more fruitful lives.

In China, according to folklore, people are asked to choose whether they would save a baby or an older woman, if both were drowning at the same time. Surprisingly to many in our culture, the Chinese would choose the older woman. Their reasoning is quite simple – while the young life is precious, the older woman has irreplaceable wisdom. And indeed, in all my years of studying health, the most valuable lesson I've learned is to follow great women mentors, wherever I find them, for they are our greatest wealth.

I now proudly share the following stories from my wonderful mentors to shake up your life, to help you claim all that is yours.

Part I:
Healers Speak Out

General Clara Adams-Ender's
Rise to the Stars

"I always had an answer, and I always
answered the question."
~ Gen. Clara Adams-Ender, US Army

Looking back, it's still hard to believe I was in the Army during
the Vietnam War. Soldiers were forty to a ward, heads wrapped,

limbs missing. The terror of my first time surrounded by war's havoc remains indelible.

Thankfully, there was, as there often is, a saving grace. Her name was Major Clara Adams.

Back then she was our Medical Surgical nursing instructor at Walter Reed. From the moment she walked us onto those wards, her modeling was our greatest gift. Forty-plus years later, I feel fortunate to have been her student during such a crucial time.

She showed us how to not be afraid, lighting up the ward whenever she entered. Not only was she an incredible medical-surgical nursing instructor, she was also an all-around great role model. Her story will show you exactly what I mean by the importance of learning from mentors.

I believe in my heart of hearts that the world is better in countless many ways, because of the spirit and work of this one remarkable leader! Sit back, relax, and enjoy.

Gen. Clara Adams Ender's Story

Once upon a time, something bad happened. I can't recall exactly when it was, but it definitely happened - health care became a big business.

The year I was born, 1939, was the year that World War II began. United Nations Day was October 1945. I still remember how

Choosing My Career

I was sure I would somehow go to college. I didn't miss more than three days of school during college years; I had missed enough classes in my life. There was a new nursing school where my sister was studying. I believed in doing what my father wanted; I felt I could always do law later. While I was at North Carolina Agricultural and Technical State University in Greensboro, North Carolina, I found, in all honesty, that nursing was not a bad profession. What I liked was that it was a challenge; I always like a challenge!

I didn't know about law, I just knew I wanted to be like those women at the top. It was the same in nursing; you had to do a lot to make it to the top. I knew where there was a will there was always a way. In my second year, I found that I needed to do something so I could stop all my little jobs. Dad was paying tuition, but there's always more that you need, and college students are always hungry.

One night I saw a sign at the student union, "Army Nurse Corps," and I thought, "Those folks must have some money." And I was right. I spoke to the Major. She said they would pay for two years and I would owe them three.

Mom was fine to sign. My dad needed some coaxing, because farmers had a ritual they went through. They would finish crops, and in the evening, go to a corner grocery store and have a beer or soda (dad didn't drink). They would sit and gossip about everything.

He told the fellows his daughter came home with papers to join the Army.

They said the only reason I was doing this was to find a man. He came home and told us this, over supper. My mother said: "There is nothing she could do in the Army that she couldn't do here. She's taking this scholarship so the other kids would have money; so just sign your name."

My dad knew to listen when my mother raised her voice. He signed my paper; they got me my scholarship.

I then had the time needed to get my class work done. They gave me tuition, room and board, plus a stipend of $250 per month. I was rich! Before graduating, they gave me a commission, and I went on active duty. I then did basic training at Fort Sam Houston.

I'd always wanted to be Roman Catholic. The minute I became active, I went to the church to get some catechism; that turned out well. I met a priest I still know today.

In the Army

I went to Fort Dix for fourteen months; then I went to Korea, do something important. I always had an answer; and I always answered the question.

Walter Reed Army Medical Center

Then I came to Walter Reed Army Medical Center. They needed lieutenants in Vietnam, so I was told to go to Walter Reed and teach lieutenants.

I was there for five years teaching the WRAIN students (Walter Reed Army Institute of Nursing), which is where I met the author of this book, when she was a young aspiring officer candidate.

Seeking Equality

When I was in college, I was active in civil rights. My school was where the first sit-ins started, at the Woolworth's lunch counter.

They would allow us to shop in stores, but you couldn't eat at the counter. It was told to me that we couldn't socialize with white folks; I couldn't understand it. So I got active in college, and stayed to make sure they got rid of Jim Crow laws.

When I first got to D.C., I noticed at WRAIN there were NO black students. I spoke with the director; I said "one of these days y'all gonna have to change these rules." D.C. was then 80% black.

I was happy to be there, teaching in that school. I knew I wanted to teach. I liked the teaching, and didn't like the salary they paid for University of Maryland instructors. I was glad the Army paid me, not them; the money I earned as a Major was 1.5 times that being paid by the university. Plus, I got great experience.

Then I did minority recruiting and pulled some more black students in. I loved my five years there and wouldn't trade it for anything. Education matters! I still believe that education is the greatest key to getting folks civilized.

I believe in my heart, that many people don't understand how important getting an education is; they miss out on so much. Sometimes, however, people who are highly educated don't exhibit good common sense.

After Walter Reed was when I really started to get into the administrative aspect of nursing practice, instead of dealing with the hands-on clinical stuff.

When I left WRAIN, I went to Ft. Meade for a year, where I was the assistant to a very good chief nurse. She told me a whole lot about administering to those folks who lay on hands every day. They determine if you will make it or not. I did a lot of paying attention.

I think that was why I did so well, because I did pay attention. I was promoted early every time, below the primary zone of my year group; I didn't even know who my group was.

I was doing very well in my profession and in the military. I was made full colonel after eighteen years of service, which usually takes folks at least 22-25 years. I was humming!

The General with US President, Ronald Reagan

And I was having a great time. I attribute a lot to having grown up with those ten kids. When we were growing, I learned a lot about how to deal with all those different personalities and characters. It served me very well to know how to get along with different types.

Overcoming Obstacles

Obstacles – what obstacles have I NOT overcome?

I learned very early how to view obstacles. Often people view them negatively; they think it's something to stop you. I don't see it like that. To me, obstacles are something you must learn how to go over, under, around, or through to get to your goal.

Someone's always willing to try to slow down your game, so it's up to you to consider whether it will be over, under, around, or through, 'cause I'm getting there.

You have to be resolved. I'll tell you, it becomes one of the greatest games you could ever play. Many times you need that obstacle to excel, and besides, life wouldn't be any fun without learning to stretch.

- I always kept my eye on the goal, knowing I would figure out how to get there.

- Persistence is key, though some days the best thing to do is go home and have a good night's sleep. Sometimes that's as important as beating on walls.

- Learning how to balance, when to use certain tools, when to stop, when to try something else. I never suffer in silence; somebody's gonna know that I'm havin' trouble. I make sure they get my message so they can help me out.

From all that I've learned, I have written my own book, *My Rise to the Stars*, where I share many of the stories in detail (www.ClaraCares.com).

At the end, I list "Clara's Aphorisms," fifteen of them, my favorite sayings, like "Whatever you do, do it with enthusiasm" and "Take yourself seriously, but not too seriously." And "Always encourage others, especially youngsters."

I wrote my book because so many folks said, "You must have been born with a silver spoon in your mouth." Now you know I wasn't.

One of my sayings is to always know what *you* expect of you. It's nice that others expect things of you, but it's what *you* expect of you that matters in this life. You've gotta get that straight for yourself.

What others expect is all right, but you'll never be disappointed if you take care of your expectations for you.

Keep Helping Others

My mom and dad were my mentors. I didn't think I could ever give up on anything. They wouldn't hear of it. They wouldn't even listen to us talk about quitting. Because of that, I probably stayed in some things longer than I should've.

I knew three boys who were sons of people I met near Dallas. Their parents were never sober, always either drunk or stoned. One day the oldest went to get some food, started stealing food from the grocery store, and got caught. The grocer said: "I know who you are. I know your situation; I won't turn you in." For the next three years he scrounged from the garbage, to feed his younger brothers.

They eventually got adopted. A family here, near me, wanted to adopt the older boy, but when he arrived, he brought all three. He said: "I been caring for my brothers since I was seven" so this couple adopted those three boys.

The dad has died; his mom is still around. Now they have a nice warm house, clothing and meals. He graduated from high school and got an appointment to West Point.

He's self-motivated, so is his youngest brother, but the middle son, Matthew, is an artist who likes drawing and cartooning, hates science, and wants to graduate high school.

I kept advising him to skip that "I hate science" thing.

Now we are working together since John went to West Point. Matthew looks at me like, "Won't you ever go away"? And I say, "Nope, I'm never going away. You're going to get through high school."

We knew that as lieutenant, my time had come and gone; it was over for me.

I met Heinz (my dear husband, a retired doctor) three weeks after I got there; I never did read those books I packed. Instead, he showed me Europe in style.

Then, I got orders to come back home and he wanted to come to America with me. We decided to get married; he wanted to help me. I can tell you this: I had kissed a lot of toads in my life; not one ever offered to help! He helped.

The General and Heinz

I had just made full colonel and had to have some assistance to do a lot of the social stuff. I needed a wife! He was a wife and more.

I brought him along to America, where we got married in Illinois. We married in 1981. He died in 2004 and I miss him. We had dated for three years and it all worked out very, very well.

He refused to clean house, but he would supervise. In Germany, doctors didn't do menial tasks. However, he supervised housecleaning, and volunteering at Army Community services, where he was very helpful.

That was a great decision I made that day, to marry that boy!

When I got to be a general, he had to join in with officers wives clubs, where he helped us raise money and do great stuff.

He had a marvelous time and I did too. The ladies loved him and I could always take him along. He took care of himself and was a great traveler.

That German-American Thing

Now there is one thing we had to conquer. Heinz was twenty-six years older than I, and had been in WWII. The Germans were then our enemies.

We had to come to some understanding. I told him that Hitler could never have won, because he was about getting rid of everyone except the master race. And that meant Hitler would have eliminated people like me, if we had let him.

We had to get all that sorted out. He had fought with the German General Rommel in North Africa, who had walked between his troops supporting them, eventually countering Hitler and then forced to commit suicide.

On Aging

Getting older is going to happen to you, if you live long enough. It's reality. That fear is an illusion. That something is going to be bad about this need not necessarily be so.

I'm having such a great time! I've never felt so free. I don't waste a lot of time with people. Either we're gonna have something here or we're not; let's move on.

I want women to know that the decision as to whether or not you are important lies within yourself.

You have to look within to determine what is important, and what the expectations are. Even making it day to day, you have to be very familiar with your body, and know if it is going to go where you want it to go.

I do exercise at least five days a week; I used to run, but now I do water aerobics, a stationary bike and Nordic Track.

For the past year or so I'm into yoga again. I've done it off and on most of my adult life. Yoga is very helpful for the "stretching" our bodies need. Exercise is a huge part of staying healthy.

Causes

I work for causes that I believe in.

I am not about to be a part of anything just to give someone the chance to say, " I tried to include "them."

I once spoke with a man who wanted me to send some children I knew to attend his school, but I wasn't sure if he was just trying to meet some quota.

I told him: "I will send you people who will be models, so our people will look like the students you are talking about. My kids may have some qualities that your kids will not have." He assured me that he would look after them personally. I told him that the folks I would send will be based on your criteria, and will be outstanding candidates for your school. He offered me a job!

Wow! Now that's something I don't need – I am hard-core unemployed. "Work" is a four-letter word to me now. Today, I have to be free to do what I need to do, every day counts. I probably won't get another seventy years. I have earned my stripes. I can say what I need to say; ain't nobody will send us to outer Slobovia.

As a General, people will always give you more to do than you have time to do it in. You do what you can, and fake the rest. Pretty soon people will think you're smart!

I think often about 9/11. A lot of those folks may have gotten up that day and forgotten to say "I love you." Once you live this way, you become so much freer. I'm having a good old time. In fact, I'm having a great time.

You need to come to grips that you are a mortal being. When we don't, we carry a fear inside us that keeps us from living fully and prevents us from claiming our whole life. We put so many obstacles in the way of people coming to grips.

Religion gets in the way, you know. We give folks ways to put off things so we don't have to face the fact that we have to do this because maybe we won't be here one day. We give them opportunities to make excuses.

On Living and Dying

I used to teach 'death and dying' classes. I have now determined beyond any doubt that I have taught right -- nobody gets out of this life alive.

If Heinz didn't live forever, nobody will. We had a great time, truly a great ride.

One of the things that cause women to have problems growing old is their fear of dying. Folks, that's gonna happen!

Just as sure as the sun came up this morning, the process of life is that we are born, we live, and we die. Don't waste time fearing it, it will happen, I assure you. Get comfy with it.

I stick close to nursing because my patients have taught me so much about living and dying, especially two groups:

1. The drunks of this world, just trying to make it one day at a time. Early in my career as an administrator, they taught me that you have to learn to fake it 'til you make it. If you wake up one day and decide you want to be sober, but you don't have the will, act like you want to be sober and don't open the bottle. Pretty soon there's no difference between fakin' it and what's real. The end result is the same; you didn't get drunk that day.

2. Terminally ill folks. They taught me don't waste time in bad relationships. Live each day as if your last, it might well be.

There are great books now on 'death and dying' including Elizabeth Kubler-Ross's work that shares how beautiful it can be. Accept that you are a mortal being and move on.

I'm not afraid of dying; I just work at living fully.

The General Today

I just got out of Russia a couple of weeks ago. It's important that we find ways to talk so we don't fight.

Next book I'll be writing will be called *More Like Myself: My Life After the Military.* It is based on a quote I use from the book *Meditations for Women Who Do Too Much.*

We grow neither better nor worse as we get old, but more like ourselves.

I just spoke in Korea in May of this year, at the demilitarized zone. It was great. They finished up their training that morning, their road march. They were so happy; they got the afternoon off. It was a thrill being able to speak with them. Forty years ago I was one of them.

I'm ready for nurses to get out of hospitals. Give patients over to the people who want to support sick care and let nurses get on with preventing illness and making people well.

My Legacy

A famous author and philosopher wrote that the "purpose of life is to count, to have made a difference that you lived at all."

When I started to think of my legacy and my worth for having inhabited this earth, I thought about how I wanted to be remembered after I was dead and gone.

I decided to embrace a cause that had been suggested to me by a protégé some years earlier. I decided to help poor students who were working their way through college to be successful in their quest for education.

If they fall short of their tuition for the semester, my foundation, the CAPE Legacy Fund, provides them with a grant for the remainder, so that they can stay in school.

I also partner with other non-profits to assist poor scholarship students who need funds to pay for books, computer equipment or lab fees.

It is rewarding work and just adds spice to my fulfilled life. I also stay connected to young people—the future of our nation.

Gladys Taylor McGarey
Living Holistic Medicine

*"As a female MD for 66 years, I must say, pregnancy
and birth are NOT illnesses; I am so against the use of
fetal monitors and similar abuses of medicine!
Women Must Be in Charge of Birthing!"*
~ Gladys McGarey, MD, MD, MD(h)

When Rich and I were young and living in Hawaii, and I was pregnant with my first, I had a very powerful dream one night. A woman with dark piercing eyes, and a graying bun looked deeply into my eyes and said, "Go to Phoenix." I had awakened Rich, shaking, so powerful was this dream. Within me a seed began to grow. Maybe it was time to leave the island.

The next thing we knew we had our belongings shipped from Hawaii to Phoenix. Rich was hired to be a GP attending home births with Dr. Gladys, who turned out to be the woman from my dream, with gray hair and the bun.

I watched Dr. Gladys one night over thirty years ago, attending a birth that lasted for twelve hours. As she hovered over the birthing woman, sweat dripping down her ageless face, I wondered where she got the strength to keep doing such unpredictable and difficult work. She explained right then, as if she heard my question that we all have infinite energy available to us at all times to accomplish our goals. We simply have to **tap into the source of infinite energy and we can accomplish anything** *we set out to do. I knew she was right; I knew that since ancient times, women have lived difficult lives without the resources we have today.*

Eventually, that night a ten pound baby was born. The smiles and joy at the end far outweighed the challenges of giving birth, even to such a large baby. I loved having the opportunity to work alongside this special woman doctor and to learn from her secrets.

Our first child, Shauna Lani, was born in Phoenix with the help of Dr. Gladys. During our time studying with her, we learned some amazingly effective and affordable natural remedies for baby and mother care. Being able to offer simple relief to my baby, as a new mother, allowed me a greater sense of efficacy and mastery; I recommend these for all mothers.

To this day, Dr. Gladys remains a blessed "auntie" to our family. Wait until you hear her story! How many of us can claim such unusual beginnings?

The "Mother of Living Medicine" Shares Her Amazing Life

My mother went into labor with me on the steps of the Taj Majal.

This resulted in a wild 24-hour car ride to the hospital in an old Ford Model T. Dad had to crank it to get it started, and off they went, riding furiously down the streets of India, where my parents were medical missionaries.

I went to Woodstock School in the Himalayan Mountains. It was started 150-200 years earlier, established for kids of missionaries stationed in India. Located at 7500 feet, the school was great. In winter we lived in tents in jungles while our parents took their medical work back to areas never reached by modern medicine.

We were the only white people they had ever seen. Locals would rub our arms to see if the color came off. Some had theories that my mother stuck us in cotton that soaked up the dark color.

Every week we moved to a new village and got to know the people there. I spoke Hindistani before I spoke English. When I go back there to visit now, within three days I'm fluent.

Our Unusual Upbringing

There were five of us children. My oldest brother is 97, my second bother died age 94, my sister is 93, I am 91 and my youngest brother is 89.

My parents were Christian. The community I grew up in was Christian. They started a home for children of leper parents. Some were Hindu, Sikh, Muslim, everything was represented there.

While the basic theology was Christ-oriented, we were exposed to different beliefs and cultural ideas, and different dietary habits, as well. Muslims couldn't eat pork, Hindus couldn't eat beef, you didn't question. It actually was wonderful having these people as my friends.

I came to the states when I was sixteen to start college and was a total misfit. I didn't know anything about this American culture. The math, the music - everything was very different.

College, War, and Rationing

In college, I was busy studying at Muskingum College in Ohio, It a small Presbyterian college, with only 700 students. It was a very good experience, especially since my sister was there during my first two years. She was a big help with the enormous culture shock I was experiencing. It was great.

I started medical school in 1941. World War II broke out in December, three months later. During my medical school years, penicillin was discovered, then steroids. It was a transitional time in the world, and certainly in my life.

Just before I went to the Women's Medical College in Philadelphia, I met William (Bill) McGarey, who was in a Navy V-12 program, whom I later married.

Everything at that time was geared toward the war; meat was rationed, tires were recapped and rationed, butter and sugar were scarce. Nylon hose were a big coup, if you could score them! We were at war, so we had to expect that. No one complained.

After War

After the war, I did an internship in Cincinnati. My husband, Bill, was then in medical school. After he finished his medical training and internship we moved to his hometown of Wellsville, Ohio.

We stayed there nine years, birthing our first two kids in Cincinnati. The next two were born in Wellsville, and the last two in Phoenix. We wanted and eventually had six children.

I remember when we came to Phoenix I met a young college student who wanted me to talk to a class about family planning. I asked to be able to do it in the daytime, since I liked to spend my evenings with my children. He said, "Oh, you have children? How many?" When I answered "Six" he never called back. I thought family planning meant you planned how many children you had!

We managed one day at time, living in a small town. Bill had a lot of house calls (this was back when doctors would go to people's homes to care for them). I got up with the kids; that was our division of labor.

While living in Wellsville, we had a wonderful German woman staying in a house behind us who ran our household. When we moved to Phoenix, we found a woman there to do that.

We always needed that kind of help, besides I had grown up that way. My mother was busy with patients. The "ayah" was our old mammy, like a second mother. We adored each other.

Bill was called back into service during the Korean War and was then discharged in January of 1955. He didn't want to return to Ohio. It was his dream to move us to Phoenix, so he moved there while I stayed in Ohio until the kids were out of school. I managed to sell my practice, and moved us all in June of 1955.

A New Beginning

By then, Bill had found out about the Edgar Cayce material. Edgar Cayce was known as "the sleeping prophet," a psychic who would go into an altered state of consciousness and get answers to health issues for people who consulted with him. When I arrived, Bill had spent time in the public library studying about reincarnation. Needless to say, I was surprised. Based on my early learning, I thought he had become Hindu. After a while, it began to make more sense to me.

We then met Hugh Lynn Cayce, Edgar Cayce's son, in 1957. We both became very interested in the Cayce material. Bill began to write a newsletter for physicians interested in the Cayce work called *Pathways to Health*.

In 1969, we were on a trip around the world with the ARE (Association for Research and Enlightenment). While in Israel, staying at a Kibbutz, Bill and I spent the night thinking: "If we took our Olive Tree Medical Group and turned it into the Edgar Cayce Medical Clinic, wouldn't that be exciting?" On the tour with us were four board members of the ARE; they liked our idea.

A Clinic Is Born

In 1969, we became the ARE clinic in Phoenix, AZ. During this time, we grew more and more interested in the philosophy of this work. Ever since we had met Hugh Lynn Cayce, Edgar's son, he had continued to say "Why don't you do something about all these medical readings?"

We initially didn't see how it made any sense. Then, a year later he'd say this again. We would repeat this conversation year after year, until finally we became more involved.

We ended up taking information from the Edgar Cayce readings, learning to work with castor oil and a great variety of modalities. What we realized was that he wasn't just talking about diseases; Cayce was speaking about energy, systems, people, and coordination – a paradigm shift that was not unfamiliar to me, for I was raised knowing what prayer, compassion, and love did in healing.

Turning Point

By this time, Bill and I had been married for forty-six years. During the last fifteen or twenty, he had hired a nurse who'd been working with us. They apparently had been having an affair during this time, which I had totally ignored and denied. People would bring it to my attention, so I would go through the motions of asking Bill, and he would deny it. In hindsight, I realize that I needed to believe him, because I felt I couldn't step up on my own. When our marriage finally did come apart, my daughter Helene was there to help me pick up the pieces and continue the practice with me.

The desert tree – when it puts roots down and hits layers of solid clay - has two choices. It can put roots out sideways, in which case it dies. Or, it can use all of its energy breaking through the clay to reach its sustaining source. I knew that. I kept my focus clear. I had work to do.

Realizing that the work was important and what I was doing was vital, as was my commitment, I was determined that this was where I was going to put my energy and not get distracted. When Bill asked for a divorce, I was shattered. I felt the world had come to an end.

I called, the actress, Lindsay Wagner, who had become a friend, and told her I felt like an old coat left hung on the peg. She reminded me that my marriage was the old coat -- not me.
My kids, friends, patients; everyone was magnificent. I worked hard, kept myself going, and eventually I got through it.

A Thanksgiving Transformation

The first Thanksgiving after our separation, our daughter Analea and son Bob were with me, as were my son John and Bobbi his wife, and my daughter Helene and her husband came with the boys. We were having a great time until I pulled out that horrible platter.

Many years prior during Thanksgiving, our platter broke right before the meal. I sent Bill out on Thanksgiving Day, and he came back with a platter with an ugly bull on it. We had used it year after year. Every time I looked at it, I hated it more.

This year, when we finished dinner, while cleaning up, Analea said, "Mom, we really need to do something with that platter."

Before we even thought about it, we got out some scarves and wrapped them around our heads. John grabbed a mallet; Bobbi (A Presbyterian minister) got her Bible. We all marched to the backyard, chanting "shamanani" (shaman nani – my grandkids called me "nani."

We all had lighted candles. John dug a hole for the platter; we danced around the hole, put the bull platter in the hole, still singing "shamanani."

I took the first whack; after me, everyone whacked it into pieces. Then we all covered it with dirt, sealed it with wax dripping from the candles, while Bobbi read from Psalm 50, Verse 9, *I will take no bull out of your house.*

We finished, sealing it up with dirt, marching our "shamanani choir" back to the house. That ceremony was important to our family and to me. It allowed something that was not acceptable any more in my life to be buried and finished.

Helene, an MD, and I joined forces and started our own practice. Bill and Peggy (his nurse) got married, but his life did not go well after that. The clinic disintegrated as he became senile; yet something beautiful happened since.

He died Nov 3, 2008. At that time, he was in hospice. Helene, her son and I went to see him on his birthday. He was coherent for a short time.

Helene had her cell phone with her and said "Dad would you like to speak to your sons?" Miraculously, he spoke with each, almost swallowing the phone in the process as he brought it closer and closer.

We left. Three days later he died. Then, on December 20, I awoke during the night about 2 am; this was the night that would have been our 68th wedding anniversary. I spent the rest of the night reliving our life.

This turned out to be my best anniversary ever.
The last twenty years was a sabbatical for each of us to learn other things, but our life together had been wonderful. We had raised a wonderful family, great children and grandchildren with much joy and laughter.

Our courtship had been magical, as were our lives together. We had climbed the Great Pyramid, gone to Cambodia, seen Stonehenge. We always had such wonderful people around our table. Reliving all of this made it such a precious and healing night.

I later told my daughter: I've just moved from karma into grace... Bill is now helping me from another plane. He is around in ways he never was on this dimension." It has been absolutely wonderful for me and for my kids.

On Meeting Life's Irritations

I feel that it is really important to keep your eye on where you're going. Don't get caught up with minutia or irritation. We all have things we could spend time being angry about, or we can look at them and move on.

My sister, two years older, and I were talking recently. I noticed that both of us had a similar habit. When speaking about something upsetting, we'd take a hand to sweep it past.

This movement was done in a sweeping manner, with hand open in front and moving it back. While it was never something we had noticed before, we realized it was something our mom had done often when we were young.

When something happened that she didn't want to stay immersed in, she'd say in Hindi – "it doesn't make any difference" – and sweep her hands to move it past her. I think that has helped me through a lot.

With the situation surrounding Bill and Peggy, I had chosen to keep my focus, not to put any energy into it. If you try to not put energy into it, if you let it come into your hand and move it past, it's gone. Then it doesn't linger on as an issue.

Gems from Gladys: A Seasoned Woman Doctor Speaks From the Heart

Finding humor in life situations is really important – life can be really funny! When I realized Bill's name William was "will I am," I got the humor, for his will became a problem for his life.

I think Bill has recently been helping with our new project "Gathering of the Eagles", doctors drawn from the pool at the Association for Research and Enlightenment from which we emerged. We called together physicians from all over the country; thirty-seven were able to attend our first meeting. We had a successful conference, working on making holistic contributions to the emerging health care paradigm our country sorely needs. We put together a paper that we then hand carried to our representatives in D.C.

Our health care system is so broken. What they're talking about politically has only to do with insurance; what we need is a far greater paradigm shift.

Instead of medicine continuing its war against disease, we feel we can now step into the process of working with people. We can kill bacteria, eradicate AIDS, and work to eliminate crucial public health threats. Yet we still use language that keeps us bound to the old way of viewing medicine. We still have "cancer support groups." Are these groups to support cancer?

To me 'anti-aging' is a joke; what else are we supposed to do?

We will be born, die, have pain, and disease, but our focus on life and how we deal with life will be our medicine. Life itself becomes the great healer.

As I'd written earlier, I was raised to believe that love is the most important aspect of healing – the modalities we use become secondary. **As doctors, we need to shift our focus to enhancing life; on living well, and strengthening from within; not only on killing germs.**

I think we, as women, have been trying to regain our power, but have been blindsided from the start in the realm of medicine. For example, what is happening in obstetrical care makes me angry! We women have been giving birth since Eve. Occasionally we need help, but pregnancy and delivery are not illnesses. Pregnancy and birth are issues where we women have completely given up our power. Women need to be in charge of birthing.

I became aware of another instance where a beautiful young

woman went into normal labor, as normal as can be. She got into the hospital and they wanted things to move faster. They acted aggressively, rupturing her membranes.

Then she was bedridden, on monitors, so naturally her contractions slowed down. Next, they started a Pitocin drip, medicine so strong that her contractions overwhelmed her, tightening her uterus constantly -- with no time in between to catch her breath.

Now, she was in real pain. They asked her, "Do you want an epidural?" Then, her monitor picked up something abnormal; so they hooked her up to an internal monitor to see if the baby was in distress.

I want it on record that, as a female MD, practicing medicine for 66 years, I am so opposed to using internal monitors, and to many similar abuses of medical care.

The place the monitor is positioned is right on the baby's crown chakra, the soft spot on the baby's head. Many eastern religions feel is the place where spirit comes into the baby during the birth process.

It is a delicate spot, one that, instinctively, mothers tell others not to touch, even after birth. In the ancient Sanskrit chakra system, the crown is the top, or the seventh chakra, having to do with our connection to our Higher Power.

What should have been a perfectly normal delivery, costing nothing, is now a profitable disease. The hospital costs, IVs, epidurals, procedures and medications are billed at many times their cost, making it a very lucrative business at the cost of the patient.

Doctors now just catch the baby, that's it. They seem to have no appreciation for the sacredness of the moment. And a nurse is attached full-time to a computerized monitor image, not with the patient, sitting outside at a desk. The doctor has one monitor in her office and another in her home. So what's wrong with this picture? To me it's simple: There is no one with the patient.

This is a perfectly monitored delivery – but where is the power? Health care is morphing into an unsustainable and overly expensive proposition, with multiple computers at all locations, special cameras and technical support – all driving up our health care costs.

We are in the mess we're in because we have taken something beautiful and glorious, something that should be a spiritual transitional experience of the soul, and we have made it into something so mechanical.

At the same time, young woman are asked to totally give up their power. I am so upset at the number of Caesarian sections being done.

We have taken Mother Nature's ability to work with us, and

made it into something pathological that must be "cured." Yet those of us in the healing realm know that "healing" (making whole all aspects of your life, including body/mind/spirit) is much more valuable to us than merely "curing" or elimination of mostly physical symptoms.

I recommend young women consider reading my book ***Born to Live*** (available through Amazon.com or InkwellProductions.com).

For medicine to become more relevant, we doctors need to consider the sacredness of life – and to recognize that, contrary to our training, which also merits review, life is not one big disease.

Healers in all arenas, and health care consumers, are continuing to reclaim that which is loving, beautiful, and empowering. Consumers can learn to pursue new ways to enhance their lives, instead of giving up power. We need to reclaim the feminine face of medicine!

My fellow Eagles and I meet regularly, growing our circle until we have a loud and strong voice that will inspire our leaders to not only change the type of insurance available to our citizens, but actually change the way they are treated.

Then I will know my work is complete.

Barbara Dossey
Nightingale Scholar and Master Mentor

"We must learn to identify what our soul's purpose is;
Our journey is to create new meaning in our lives.
Telling our stories is so important."
~ Barbara Dossey RN, PhD: FAAN
Nursing Leader, Visionary, Friend

In this chapter, it is my joy to share with you an incredible woman of power. Barbie is an amazingly unique mentor, colleague and friend. She is a stellar example of what a difference one woman can make. Known in nursing circles throughout the world, Barbie inspires others with her grace, charm, and commitment to honoring the wisdom of Florence Nightingale. For 45 years, Barbara has been married to her equally amazing partner, Larry Dossey, MD, who has written more than a dozen books on health, medicine, and the power of prayer. They are the kind of people who make others proud to know them.

I met Barbie Dossey in 1995 while attending my first American Holistic Nurses Association conference (AHNA). During the conference, I mentioned to a nurse or two that I had written <u>The Nightingale Conspiracy</u>, my book on nursing, and was seeking publication. One woman pointed out Barbie, suggesting that I speak with her. After a break, I sat down next to her and introduced myself. She was so open, so wise, and so caring that she melted my heart. And she is beautiful! The woman didn't even know me and here she was giving me the name of her literary agent, which most authors keep guarded under lock and key.

Barbie is grace under fire, overflowing with wisdom and light. Through decades, she has inspired thousands with her passion for nursing. She is tiny, but powerful. And that is the image I seek to share in this book. Women have a different strength, one that is essential to our equilibrium. It is a strength that, when missing, makes the world seem sad and off-balance.

Today Barbie is International Co-Director of the Nightingale Initiative for Global Health (NIGH), a holistic nursing pioneer, a Florence Nightingale scholar, a nurse theorist, Co-Director of the International Nurse Coach Association, and Co-Director of the Integrative Nurse Coach Certificate Program (INCCP). Also, as a recognized elder in the AHNA, she is helping to guide the association toward a bright future. Largely due to her heroic efforts.

Holistic Nursing was recognized as a nursing specialty by the American Nurses Association in 2006 and each year a hundred nurses take the national holistic nursing certification examination. As board-certified holistic nurses (caring for body-mind-spirit, holistically) we are expanding our roles in health care and in healing the Earth, as well.

Knowing Barbie has shown me of the limitless nature of our beings. I have woven her passion into my life quilt and can always call forth her spirit. This tiny woman is a Master Teacher, beautiful inside and out. She is so caring for our world; and such a lovely model of caring. Thank you, Barbie, for shining your light on this world; lighting our way to better health care.

In 2010, Barbara Dossey received the prestigious Leadership Award at the Leadership Health Care Symposium, honoring a pioneer whose leadership and compassion have shaped integrative healthcare and the nursing profession. We who know her are honored. Congratulations Barbie!

Barbie's Story

I grew up in the South, blessed to have a wonderful family. We had a lively household and our house was always full of friends.

I had three older cousins who were nurses, and I loved hearing the stories of their work. When we went to family reunions to visit, I saw them in their nursing uniforms, with blue capes and nursing caps. I am sure that this nursing image got into my psyche.

Their father insisted that all three become nurses as they would be able to travel, be independent, and would always have a job. So I developed a sense of what nurses did. Growing up in the 1950s, I wasn't around many working women, but my nursing cousins demonstrated the joy in being professionals, with responsibility for others.

At a family reunion in my junior year of high school, my uncle asked what I planned to do with my life. When I told him I wasn't sure, he told me I'd make a really good nurse. The next week I had a meeting with my high school counselor, who also felt that I would be a good nurse. My aptitude tests indicated this as well. So off to college I went.

Education and Experience

During my junior year of college, the first open heart surgery was performed at Baylor University Medical Center in Dallas. I fell in love with critical care nursing. I attended my first nursing theory conference within months of completing nursing school. When I heard these theorists who were truly helping to shape the philosophy of nursing, I was hooked. This became the focus of my career.

In 1965, I acquired a recurrent viral infection after eating contaminated food in Mexico. I had a terrible fever with related symptoms. Within 24 hours I had an eruption of a fever blister on my cornea that resulted in my needing a corneal transplant in 1975. There is still a risk of this recurring. This is where my personal self-care strategies and wellness focus have assisted me in staying healthy. This experience infused my nursing work.

I became clear on one key message: life's journey is about healing.

Healing is a lifelong journey, wherein we seek wholeness, harmony and balance in the way we live our life, with family and friends, with co-workers, and with new partnerships globally. As with any worthwhile journey, it starts with a small step. Each step leads us closer to a more whole, balanced life. Take yours today!

A Calling

I was called to holistic nursing, to exploring the life of Florence Nightingale, and to engage in global nursing. I didn't plan this, but as I was alert to nursing and its role in creating a healthy world, I began to wonder why so many are disenfranchised and having such a tough time.

We currently are living in a culture of scarcity, fear and nasty politics. Sadly, this is how our world has changed. We each have a responsibility to address our suffering.

It starts with identifying our own pain. We all have suffering; it is a part of the human condition. But we must understand and accept that this is the journey of life.

We must acknowledge our story and learn to process the pain.

Suffering has purpose, and can provide new meaning. Mute suffering is when people keep telling themselves the same story "nothing will change around here, there's never going to be enough time." These people just put in their 8-12 hours shifts. They do not claim their full power.

The Power of Our Story

Telling our stories is so important. We can come together to build community. To really be heard, we must have others who can bear witness to our story.

As we feel safer to share our deepest pain, we come to another level, one that allows us to express our suffering.

In this way, we also learn about the suffering of others and how it relates to our own lives. Then, as we travel on, we bring their strength and knowledge with us on our journey, having discovered new identities and meanings in our personal and collective suffering. It allows us to gain insight, invoking our intuition. We can then enjoy the present moment, cherishing a beautiful sunset, or rejoicing in a child's laughter. Our joy emanates as we watch the sun disappear, or laugh with the child.

We need to remind each other to take these precious moments during our day. These "trans-personal experiences" of taking a minute to look at the sky, or other special moments in time, evoke symbolism. They truly help us to connect beyond ordinary limits and boundaries of our lives, reminding us of that which is larger, and encompasses us all.

We need to ask "What is the story we're telling ourselves?" No one can interpret your pain and suffering. Whatever the issue, we must realize there are signs and symptoms—physical, mental, emotional, social, behavioral and spiritual.

You may think you're doing a good job of covering up your pain, but a trained and healthy nurse can sense it.

When I see burned-out, depleted nurses, I have come to believe they are feeling anguish over something they are unable to accomplish. When nurses are prevented from doing their best, there is suffering. Nurses come to nursing with a dream. Some may also come from painful backgrounds which must be healed. The current system presents many threats to our composure, balance and integrity.

Each of us wants to do her/his absolute best. However, when a negative story keeps repeating in one's head, awareness of the present moment is diminished, as is our ability to make healthy choices.

That is exactly where our self-care practices such as meditation, stress management, and eating nutritiously, can assist us. We can learn to identify our soul pain, distinct from the pervasive cultural pain. There is a lot of pain in our culture. We are becoming increasingly alienated from the deepest part of who we are.

No one can reconnect us *except* us.

We can find soul mates and others to help us along the path, but it is always our job to heal our selves. Holistic nursing teaches us that in promoting health for others, we have to do the same for ourselves. We must learn to acknowledge the aspects in ourselves that require attention, and to care for ourselves.

So many times our life doesn't go the way we want it, yet

later these experiences become our teachers. I once didn't get a job as a head nurse though I really wanted it, and I became demoralized. But, two weeks later, I was invited to be on a grant with a medical project to take returning Vietnam veterans and teach them to become Associate Degree nurses. It was a joyful experience I would not have missed! I believe that when one door closes, another opens.

Another key is **our intention.** This is where I have found the clearest direction. I find that I must start with a deep intention about the work I'm doing. It's that conscious awareness of being in the present moment, knowing that I must do what I've been called to do, that brings me back time and again to my intention. It is a truly deep love that happens in that space, by setting my intention and coming into awareness.

Today

I'm 69 now, and I love it. Life is so much fun. Now we are like women in their 40s used to be -- it's said that sixty is the new forty -- and I feel the best is yet to come. I am aware that when I operate out of abundance, I feel the blessings and am more able to practice letting go of attachments to this life. I believe that practicing this meditation will be helpful when my transition comes.

I like to be able to weave wisdom together, mentoring young nurses, sharing the joy. I didn't have a formula for pulling my life together, but I did realize some important steps along the way.

Having expressive and creative forms of art is important. My art form is needlework; I am an avid needle-pointer and almost always have two or three projects going at the same time. I am also blessed; my husband loves needlework as much as I do. We often stitch on each other's projects while watching videos. I find that if I don't stitch at least every three or four days, I lose my balance and find work difficult. I even find it therapeutic, as I solve so many challenges while I pull the thread in and out of the canvas.

I also love oriental flower arranging that is called ikebana. Another healing ritual is a long hot soaking bath that can be elevated to an art form with candles, burning incense, and a cup of tea. I also realize I am feeling a need to slow down and play a little more.

One of the rich joys of my life is my girlfriends. Karilee and I met at Mills College. Sitting by each other, she showed me her book; I gave her the name of my agent. She reached out, touched me with her story, and as we joined forces we supported each other's work. This simple act of joining hearts is what helps to make us whole, keeping our work flowing at deeper and deeper levels.

Barbie Dossey and the editor

Gems from Barbie:

- *Now it is clear that we are a global village.* Whatever I do personally does impact the greater whole. Holistic nursing, with its focus on weaving together threads of various aspects of our selves (physical, mental, social, emotional and spiritual) restores us to wholeness.

- *The processes of recovery, repair, and renewal are transformative. Transformation is what healing is about.* We all go through changes and transformation in our lives. There are times I have thought one direction was right for me, but then it didn't feel right, so I'd have to make course corrections.

- *We must learn to identify what our soul's purpose is, rather than resent what we're doing.* We must become more aware of our feelings, our desires, and our abilities. We can use many tools to help us be more reflective; this quiet time is where we gain insight and new awareness of what is vital.

- For me, I like to use imagery and relaxed breathing exercises, take walks in nature, do needlepoint, meditate, burn incense, and ask myself, *"What is it I want to tell others?"*

- Many women have discovered true joy by becoming involved in the transformative process. Creative women can easily get bored (as reading about women in past times confirms). *We must live on an edge, pushing ourselves to listen to that "tug from within" that calls us now.*

- *We are constantly in motion, as the physics of molecules tells us.* Florence Nightingale called her work her "must." When we identify our "must" we are on fire, working from soul's purpose.

- The process is one of learning to establish right relationships within all aspects of our selves, *allowing our body-mind-spirit-and environment to interact in a healthy manner.*

- *The journey is about inner knowing.* We don't know everything, but learning about small aspects that pique our interest can help us along the way.

- *Stay steady and focused on the endeavor now.*

- Our journey allows us to *create new meaning* in our lives.

- *Joy in living can arise from daily rituals of healing.* Taking 10-15 minutes to sit in meditation each day can make a world of difference. Why? Our minds are busy; we must organize, becoming more clear and focused. Creating rituals of healing allows us to enter sacred space. Then we are able to honor who we are. In those moments, we move to the core of our humanity and remember how connected we are, that we are not in this world alone; that we are part of a greater whole.

- *Rituals of healing help us remember to connect with those invisible forces that allow us to have meaning, depth and structure in our lives.* That repetitive breathing, in and out, connects us to the past and future. We can then let go of old ways of being, thinking, and behaviors that have kept us stuck. Now we integrate.

- *We cannot operate out of scarcity. We must live our lives from a feeling of abundance.* Even if we have little, we can focus on what we do have, and magnify its effects. Soon we have more, and we can continue to give gratitude for what we do have, instead of focusing on what we lack.

Barbie and Larry Dossey

To read more on Barbara Dossey see:
http://www.dosseydossey.com and http://inursecoach.com

Shalamah Yahchove, D.C.
Woman of Spirit and Transformational Healer

"One beautiful thing that I can share with you,
About my poor socio-economically deprived people,
They NEVER EVER taught me to hate,
no matter what happened."
~ Dr. Shalamah

I want to share a beautiful woman with you, someone I met during my personal times of need.

I sense that I may have more bodily aches and pains than many others; though I may never know whether or not this is true. Unusual about my body is that while it was forming, inside the uterus of my mother, she was stricken with polio (which apparently does cross the placental barrier). She had excruciating headaches, which I was also plagued with for much of my adult life. I consider massage a way to help my body keep going, feel better, and perform at is optimal level. I am a dancer as well, and massage truly helps.

Some massage therapists do a good job, but Dr. Shalamah Yahchove is in another category altogether. Her name, "Shalamah," means perfection. She is the woman who touches me when I need massage at my favorite hot springs, in the mountains in California; her touch has inspired my soul. While I have been receiving massage regularly for my healing since age 27, this is one woman whose touch worked miracles for me.

She is not only a massage-touch-therapist, she is also a D.C. (Doctor of Chiropractic), a course of study that takes 4-years to complete. But she didn't stop learning there. She also has learned from native healers in various parts of the world. I remain deeply grateful for her wisdom as it is shared here.

Meet Dr. Shalamah

Greetings! My name is Dr. Shalamah Yahchove.

I have had many years of study and strict discipline in the fields of massage and chiropractic. I currently practice at Wilbur Hot Springs, in Sacramento, and in Berkeley, CA. I tailor my massage and chiropractic treatments, meeting the needs of each individual patient, assisting on their healing journey. In addition to my chiropractic and massage training, I have also studied with the indigenous Maori of New Zealand.

My approach when working with the body is to shift and release those "stuck" patterns. I am a chiropractor by trade and I specialize in deep, corrective and, restorative manual orthopedic massage work.

Now Let Me Tell You What I Really Think!

We are the Goddess, all of us beautiful women.

My village is your village; there is no separation. The truth is that "aha" we get from knowing each other's stories, recognizing that your story is mine.

Much of my wisdom has been passed down to me in nonverbal ways from my ancestors. It has all been their inspiration, their prayers, their shoulders. I stand on the shoulders of these beautiful people who gave me life.

Without my parents, grandparents, and great grandparents, and the women I saw who perform the work, I would be nothing. I am not going to accept accolades other than my offer to give back to them. It was their prayer!

I am now sixty-one years old. One circumstance I hear in practice, and in chatting with younger women, is that they don't understand the beauty of the goddess emerging. There has been a longstanding fight to control her. In her passages and beyond menopause, they try to control her nature.

But that will never work! When the goddess starts to rise, women have often been encouraged to tamper her down with drugs. That is not the correct response to her emergence; that's just the goddess coming up in her heat. That's the groundwork she leaves behind.

I encourage all women to honor our lives more fully as women, to understand our gifts, and to use them with love.

The People I Came From

I am Southern, from middle Georgia, born into a family of sharecroppers. These were people who knew the art form of farming, people who used their hands to feed their babies and feed their neighbors. They also opened their hearts to people in the community.

During the early 50s in the South, Jim Crow laws were very much in place. I experienced women in my family being afraid for their sons, husbands, and brothers; the men often left home and didn't come back. Back then, bus stations and some stores had a *colored only* water fountain and a *whites only* water-fountain and black people had to go to the back of the bus.

I saw and experienced a lot of fear. But I also saw people banding together both spiritually and politically. There weren't homeless, except for the hobos who seemed to have freedom to travel. The church members would make sure the mothers down the road with children and no husband had food to eat. I recall a "society fund," monies collected to bury the dead. These folks used their hands in planting and canning. They understood the seasons.

My people were very spiritually oriented; they practiced Christianity but also practiced a form of "voodoo," another type of spirituality. We hardly ever went to doctors, partly because the white doctors wouldn't take us, but also because my family was proactive in keeping us healthy. My mother had nine children. When we were ill, she went out and dug up herbs, such as garlic, to heal us. Each fall and winter we were given a huge dose of castor oil to help stave off the cold and flu. We just didn't have a lot of colds or sickness.

I am from the clan of people who used their hands, to grow, heal and nurture. I didn't understand some of their expression of love when I was young, for they always smiled. I have a huge family;

there are many family members that I don't know. My mother was one of fifteen kids; my father one of thirteen.

One beautiful thing that I can share with you about my poor socio-economically deprived people: they **never, ever** taught me to hate, no matter what happened.

When I could read and understand some of the social happenings and some of the violence against black folks, I just couldn't understand their smiles. This expression of smiling in the face of danger and adversity, just wouldn't compute in my brain.

"You've gotta be kiddin' me," I remember saying more than once.

I often wondered how these older and wise folks could maintain their smiles, their abilities to give and love under such dire circumstances. My mother had to go out and work hard all day long in white people's homes, then come back and take care of her children.

In my opinion, we now live in a "me" society. And in this culture, we can be seen as separate. Poverty makes people network! If I have butter and others have eggs, we have to share.

That Black/White Thing, Back When

I clearly recall, I was about four years old, my mother had gone out to do some work, the white woman she worked for drove my mother back home. My mother was sitting in the back seat; the dog was in front seat.

It seemed odd to me and I didn't understand. My mother and I never talked about it.

During my journey, I have had many conversations with people across cultures. My ability to work in this way comes from this early life.

There have been times, as I worked with some white women, it seemed to me that they wanted to speak from a deep place within, what it was for them to have a black woman take care of them in the early years of their life.

I would search for the edge to find ways to communicate with these women. "How do I do this, and be loving to you, knowing you had a black mammy?"

I posed questions to them: "Where is she? Who was this person that raised you? Did she get lost? Did you not go into the church and community and search for your black mother? Did your family not take out Social Security on them? Did you inquire with their children? Can you go back now and see if she is still alive? Can you make an altar; and offer up prayers for her and her family?" I realized that this sad legacy is a part of our shared story. I say, "Now you are an adult, you can do things to feel better about yourself, things you could not control when you were a child."

When I use massage and chiropractic to help women heal, I also realize that I only have a short window of time to help them feel better. My goal is to help these women overcome their guilt about not staying in touch with the women who cared for them. Now, I offer necessary life changes so their body and mind can function optimally.

Let's be truthful and honest; empowerment is about how we take care of all our beautiful sisters. When the queen is happy the whole land is happy. When I was growing up, there seemed to be a shortage of men; men have been the major breadwinners. I wish we could find better ways in our culture for all women to be taken care of. We need to be asking "What is it that other women need?"

Childhood Confusion

I did not have a lovely childhood; there was a lot of confusion on many different levels.

One lack of understanding was when I was in church, and saw the statue of Jesus. I didn't know what that meant. Later in life, celebrating Christmas and Santa Claus left me in a state of bewilderment. This magical time that I had wrapped my head around was a falsehood. Santa did not come down the chimney 'cause we grew up in the sticks. And I couldn't figure out why when he came to our house, presents were always very meager.

I saw and experienced abuse; incest that was leveled on me and spousal abuse by father on our mother. My siblings and I had to deal with abuse and alcoholism. I also was pregnant at fifteen. It was 1968, and there were no abortion rights that I was aware of in the state of Georgia. I question sometimes, wonder still, not being sure of the answer, if I had the choice, would I have had an abortion. This choice was not on the table in 1968.

My son was born severely mentally-challenged, and is now 44 years old. I didn't have that fun time early in life, for I went from being a "good girl" catching butterflies to dodging my father's fingers, to being a mother. I surmise that I knew nothing!

Of course, I figured at first I must be cursed getting pregnant the very first time I had sex, but I also didn't know better. No one gave me any tools to keep me from getting pregnant, or told me "if I did this then that would happen." My mother was wonderful, God bless her, but "the birds and the bees" education just wasn't there.

Another Option

I now understand that I could have just run away at 15. Instead of running, I thought that I needed to have another reason to leave the abusive home life. I became pregnant.

What I learned from that is how important it is to have family. The women came and saw that my son wasn't functioning right; they helped me to see.

My mother pushed us in every way to finish school. In the 1950s, finishing high school was a peak goal. My parents had a third grade education, my grandparents less. Finishing high school was necessary. I offer my thanks to my family for their wisdom.

My family was unhappy with me being pregnant; I didn't want to marry. A mental growth spurt happened because I wanted to finish school. So, I left Georgia and went to Miami, taking my son with me. I stayed with an Aunt who said we could come. I had many reasons to leave Georgia! Georgia had a blue law, stating that if you're pregnant, you couldn't return to school and finish your education.

I wasn't considered smart, or dumb; I now realize that I was what the system had set up for me. For instance, from first to eleventh grade, we had hand-me-down books from the white students from the white school. And even though mama had something cooking upon our return from school, many days my siblings and I went to school hungry. Now you tell me, how can any child learn when hungry? This is one challenge of living in poverty.

The good, and at times, fun part of growing up was that I lived in nature; I saw the stars at night, ate the organic food we grew, and drank water from a natural spring.

Education

As I was completing high school in Florida, my sister came for a weeklong visit and took my son back to Georgia with her. She saw that I couldn't go to school and care for him.

So I finished high school and went to the Junior College, accomplishing all that my parents and community dreamt for me. Junior Colleges at that time were hiring black teachers.

In elementary school, junior high and high school, I had only black teachers. During my senior year, there was only one white student that came to our school. This was 1970; he looked very much out of place.

I got a scholarship to Florida A & M but decided to go to the local Junior College. I was assigned to read the *Autobiography of Malcolm X* and also about Martin Luther King. As I discovered my love for reading, I also discovered that Malcolm X "turned my lights on" (not Chaucer!).

My former education had not prepared me for college, so I had to do many remedial classes to bring me up to speed for college. I felt going to the junior college was important and a good choice, being close to home. I figured that I must take what's offered, go for it, then step higher and keep stepping.

I think it may have been Oprah who said, "we have diamonds in our backyards, we have to go out and troll for them." Oprah also said that "your crown is set, pick it up, put it on."

Healing My Life

I became very radical in my first two years of junior college, because I continued to experience some white people who were cruel. I was poor and deprived because of the poverty I experienced, the hangings I knew happened, and the incest in and around my life. No one informed me that I had the ability to acquire and apply knowledge and skills, or that my ancestors were brilliant. I didn't know then that in my DNA runs the blood of brilliant people.

That was my quilt to start; I continue to weave and stitch it together.

My parents had taught me not to hate people, but I felt angry. I understood I had a journey; I needed to find my purpose. I wondered how to go forth?

All this led me to massage. I was stressed out trying to make life happen. Still fighting poverty, not realizing I had riches. I wanted to know my life's purpose and how to move forward. I wrote affirmations, I prayed, I believed and stepped out on faith.

No one told me enough that I was beautiful! The chatter at times was about good hair and bad hair. Recently, Chris Rock interviewed black women and black men about their hair. Bell

Hooks wrote about being "nappy." The journey continues! How could I feel beautiful in a system that tries to make me white?

I had to learn to uncover my beauty and my brilliance. I thought about my ancestors, transported against their will to this country and other countries from Africa in ships. I realize, and say many times over, that without my ancestors' survival skills, love and willingness to experience the journey (they could have jumped overboard the transporting ships, as some did) I would never be here.

But hey, I'm here. How beautiful is that? I'm honored. I love the process of the journey, which is your journey and everyone's journey.

My Journey Continues!

I'm so ecstatic when I wake up each morning. I know my life will never be as bad as it was, and that I have less time to live now than I have lived; now that's the glory. This I know!

I can, at times, have less tolerance for people who don't understand that the sun sets, and the sun rises, on us all. And when it rains, it rains on us all. This is part of the beautiful journey. This I know! *Ashe!*

The indigenous people of New Zealand taught me their art form of connecting to my God Self through their bodywork. This touch therapy was very deep, intense and had a quality that touched me very deeply.

Why was this? I asked the Shaman Papa Joe. He replied "Shalamah, we choose our healers at birth. We place them into our healing community very young, before three years old. By the age of nineteen, they are master body workers. Papa Joe noted further "any tight spots in your body are considered a breach of contract with your higher God Self."

That is the level the Maoris work from; we can work on this level as well. We need to rewrite our mental, physical and spiritual contracts to be all that we can be.

Gems from Dr. Shalamah Yahchove

- *We need to stay active always!*

- *Dance! Let your soul express and heal.*

- *Keep learning from others.*

- *We need a way to get us together; all of us women.* We belong together.

- *Once we realize who we are as individuals, and learn that we are goddesses, given the opportunity we must elevate our status and work on our God Selves.* Then we will have the power to change.

- *I'm seeing more soulful white people these days;* I dance with them. It's about understanding the love, not hesitating to impart that. I bless all women.

- *If I could just be 1/10th of what my mama was, I would be great.* I bless these women who called me forth to experience this life!

Venus Ann Maher, D.C.
Chiropractic, Creativity and Kindness

"Menopause helped me get real!"
~ Venus Maher D.C.

I met this next Real Hot Mama standing in front of our local food market in the small town of Cotati, CA. It's a tiny town, home of

Sonoma State University, with many students and young people, all keeping it lively.

It was love at first sight. Venus is darling, so open, loving and kind. I knew then that my long distance trips to chiropractors were over. Her office was three blocks from our house and I could walk on a peaceful bike path to get there.

Venus blends in with the community yet stands out when you are availing yourself of her services. Her work is gentle, peaceful, and intuitive. I walk out feeling like I'm floating on air.

Dr. Venus Maher came to chiropractic care early in her life. As a fifteen year old she injured her back working on a Christmas tree farm and was helped by a compassionate chiropractor. That experience ultimately led to her decision to become a doctor of chiropractic. It fit her desire to work in an alternative, independent, yet licensed field in which she can make a difference in people's lives every day.

Venus learned compassion through her suffering as a child, creating an intense desire to alleviate suffering for others. Transforming her own experience of pain turned her into the healer she was meant to be. Though she would not wish it on anyone, she would not change a moment of her childhood because it made her the doctor, mother and person she is now.

She attended Santa Rosa Junior College, Sonoma State University then graduated from Life Chiropractic College West in 1986. Venus has been taking care of her patient's medical needs ever since.

My normally happy extroverted personality deserted me, leaving a tired, emotionally fragile stranger in her place. I would cry at the oddest moments, even into my swimming goggles at the gym. My hot flashes raged, and a full night's sleep was a rarity.

At first I tried herbs, acupuncture, counseling, and natural progesterone. Nothing. I flashed on and off like a damn Christmas tree. I wept.

We mamas spend all these years putting ourselves together; then menopause takes it apart.

Recently I took a workshop on midlife with Dr. Jett Psaris and Dr. Marlena S. Lyons, who wrote the book *Undefended Love*. They confirmed my suspicions, that in midlife there is yet another disconnect, a time – as in our teens – when we are stripped of the comfort of our identity.

During this time we are left wandering in the unknown, asking "Who am I now?" and "Where is this leading me?" That was my experience.

The Crone

The answer is that the next level is the outspoken crone.

The word "crone" is sometimes used in a derogatory way to insult a woman, but it also means a woman over 40. Women over 40 can use it in an approving way, from one beautiful aging woman to another.

When I realized that I had been holding so much inside, I told myself "I'm too damn hot to be codependent." I began allowing myself to speak my truth, without the filter of the "good girl."

It wasn't always pretty. I also found that people could hear me better if I listened to their sometimes-difficult truth. I learned to show up, to be present for whatever needed to be communicated.

Menopause helped me get real.

I was simply too hot and too tired to defend myself with outdated patterns, so they fell away. It was not a happy process, but it was a necessary one.

Speaking out helped, but I needed something more. I sat down and prayed for answers. The next day I walked into the library and found *The Women's Retreat Book* by Jennifer Louden. I used it as my Bible during peri-menopause, discovering that the answers were all inside of me.

Jennifer's book said you can retreat for an hour, a day, or a week. You can do it in your home, a bookstore, a park, a friend's house, or at a Bed & Breakfast. I find going away for two to five days works best in my life. I learned to notice what I am longing for, to create an intention from that desire. Then, I turn that intention into a question. My retreats have been guided by questions such as "How can I be kind to myself?" or "How can I connect with my highest self, right now?"

On that first retreat, I asked the questions, and found wonderful creative juices getting stirred up. I made beautiful collages, wrote songs, and just had creative energy welling out of me.

Crone Years

In our earlier years, many women give birth to children. As a Crone, however, we shift to another level. Now we are giving birth to creations, not human children. We are giving back to life.

My retreats taught me to slow down. In slowing down, I discovered that even thoughts that I felt were intolerable could be processed, by taking that kind of time. You may say, "I don't have that kind of time." I understand. What I want you to know is that you can do this over your lunch break. Find what you're longing for. Then give it to yourself.

Choosing Your Own Therapies is Empowering

The second tool that helped me to recover on all levels was homeopathy. My hot flashes went from 30 a day to almost none, and my mood swings began to calm down after my homeopathic practitioner found the right remedies.

Most people reading this may not realize that homeopathy is an incredible health care modality, first recognized in Europe. The predominant allopathic medical system in the United States addresses *crisis intervention.* It operates mostly on the "I only believe what I can see" theory. And while this scientific method is valuable, it is also limited.

Our deepest feelings, and even physical reactions, operate at very subtle levels, which we can't measure, but we sure can feel in our bodies. You can also sense it in your soul; we know when there's a shift happening.

Through homeopathy and retreats, I went from peri-menopausal angst of "nobody loves me" to "we're good again." And I am grateful.

Subtle physical changes, which may not show up in lab tests, are *absolutely* real, and important! We can feel the change, as I did with homeopathic treatment in my peri-menopausal journey, and that is what truly matters.

Now I have a greater sense of the infinite. I believe I can do anything I set my mind to. The early years were hard, but I gained a deep sense of what is possible.

As a Chiropractor, I feel joy every day. When I have worked with a person, and there is that smile afterwards that shows they just dropped about thirty pounds of pain, I feel an immense honor to be a part of their healing journey. My focus is on healing the physical body, but my patients say they also feel so much better spiritually. The question in my heart is always "how can I serve you, how can I best love you?"

The answer always comes if I listen. I love making a difference in my patients' lives. I will do this until I can't walk through my office doors, which hopefully means for at least another twenty-five years.

Hafiz, the Persian poet, says (paraphrased) "If God is a divine chess master, where would all the pieces be? That's exactly where they are in your life." Spirit, and my experiences thus far, have made me who I am. I love being me.

I wouldn't change the past; it led me to this incredible life I live today.

Venus, On Inner Work

The work I've done is to dive into the heart of my pain, passing through resistance, to find the wholeness underneath. Then I get to have all my feelings, including the joy. As soon as I touch my center I find my joy. My little girl inside knows how to create, celebrate, and love.

By turning toward that which I want to run from, by using therapy and journaling, I get myself back, my whole self. I discovered that all my life I had tried to paint niceness on top of sorrow, grief and fear. It didn't work. I had to go toward my inner landscape; there's a beautiful mountain and lake inside of me. There are places to cry and places that make me laugh aloud.

Figuratively speaking, I used to live in tunnels. Now I live in a gorgeous house on top of a hill, filled with light and music, from which I can see views in every direction. There are water gardens and fern gardens and flower gardens which feed my soul. This internal place sustains me, giving me the resources to help me flourish in my outer life.

Let That Creative Child Out

Creativity has been a huge healer for me. When I was thirteen, I had an incredible teacher. I learned song-writing, so everything within me could come out in song. He taught me poetry, explaining that it turned the faucet on, and let it all pour out, whatever it was. Once it came out, things changed.
Now I teach middle school kids the same process. I give them permission, they write the songs, and we sing them. I started pottery early, and silk painting. Now I'm writing a novel! I dove into photography when my son was a baby, and that has evolved into doing family portraits and weddings.

Let the creative come through you, in images, words, dance or song. When it does come through, get out of your own way.

My happiest moments are when I'm feeling really connected,

to nature, spirit, myself, and other people. These experiences allow something to come through me that make me want to cry with joy.

I love helping people to feel better; it gives me such great uplifting. I find that both chiropractic and creative endeavors (such as song-writing, and silk-painting) are about letting something good come through me, something greater than myself. When I am part of that good, and connected to it, I feel right.

Of course, like everyone, I get sad, upset, and grumpy. But I don't stay there. I keep a seven-page list of things that make me happy nearby, and I can always find one thing to do that will make me feel better, whether it is meditation, journaling, or calling a friend. Every problem we experience is one where we forget we are always connected to something good/God. These reminders are infinitely helpful.

Women's Circles and Spiritual Journeys

When I was fourteen, we performed all night singing circles based on the Native American Peyote tradition, which broke my heart open. I ended up loving everyone around me, seeing that we're all made of the same stuff; we carry the same wounds and we are really all connected.

More recently I was longing for deep connections with women and I used the book ***Wisdom Circles*** to create a group where we speak and listen from the heart. We have been meeting every month for seven years now, and those two hours are some of the best hours I spend. It creates magic when we show up in such a real way.

I am a member of The Threshold Choir, which was started about 13 years ago by a special woman named Kate Munger. We now have over 100 choirs with approximately 1500 women involved internationally (www.thresholdchoir.org).

We sing for people on the thresholds of life – for newborns and for those who are struggling with life, which is an incredible honor.

Spiritual Journey

My spiritual journey has been a gathering process.

I started as a Catholic, then I explored Native American traditions, Buddhism, and Paganism. Twenty years ago I found the Center for Spiritual Living, which is an open place that reminds me of the greatest truths from all of these traditions.
The Center for Spiritual Living, founded by a man named Ernest Holmes, uncovers common threads that run through all great religions. It is actually more of a philosophy than a religion.

Some of the basic tenets are: There is one Creative Force, of which we are all a part. We all have direct access to God. Our body's die, but our souls live forever. To change your life, you must change your thinking. We determine what is real by finding out what is true in our life, not from what others tell us.

I kept taking classes because I didn't want to stop growing. I thus became a licensed prayer practitioner, helping others to heal the illusion of separation. This is what causes us so much pain. Healing arises from remembering that we are each a part of the great mystery and of the whole. The answer is in remembering who we are. As I pray for others, I remember who I am as well. It is a process and evolution.

Motherhood

My son, Aaron, is now seventeen. Being his mother teaches me to let go of expectations. The picture perfect Mom in the rocking chair was an illusion that set me up to feel like a failure. I changed my idea of success in a day spent with a colicky baby, learning to "feed him/feed me, clothe him/clothe me, and bathe him/bathe me." Then I had lowered the bar enough! The dishes were a plus at that point.

Of course it got easier, but he has never stopped being my teacher. Once I was rushing him into the house when he was about four, and he said "can't we stop and look at the flowers?" Another day we were beginning to escalate during that cranky pre-dinnertime. I looked at my little boy and said, "Calm down." Then I realized that he was mirroring me. As the adult, I was the one who needed to chill. I sat down on the floor and took a few deep breaths. Aaron immediately came over and got in my lap. I sang him a song, and the rest of the evening was fabulous.

The years went by and it just got better. We sailed through his fourth through twelfth year. Then came junior high and the struggles about homework and grades. He went from straight A's in sixth grade to barely making it in seventh. By the end of middle school I was dreading the impending challenges about high school grades. I talked to other parents, reading and journaling about it, coming to understand that I was too involved in his business.

Aaron and I took a kayak trip on a summer day before his freshman year of high school, and I asked him "How would you rate our relationship without grades and homework?" His answer was "Nearly perfect." We decided then that his grades were his job; I would stay out of it. If he got C's and D's it was still his job, but I was more involved. He liked the plan, and on the whole it's working. Occasionally I have to apologize to him for overstepping the boundaries of our agreement. He's very mature now.

Marriage

My spouse and I have been together for twelve years. During our third year we had an amazing wedding ceremony. We wrote our own vows and spoke them into the sacred space of friends and family. Those 130 dear ones witnessed and blessed our love, even if the world at large doesn't yet recognize our union, since we are two women in love.

I told her "I choose you, out of all the people in the world to be my beloved" and then I heard her say those same precious words to me. We continue to choose each other every day of our lives together.

I find love works best if I am not living in the past or future.

Since my family of origin was highly dysfunctional, I sometimes try to find security in a Disney-like version of reality. One of my vows was to let go of my picture of how it supposed to be, so I can be open to what actually is. When I have an idealized vision of what things are supposed to look like, I find it can get in the way of true intimacy and interaction. I have to stop, listen and arrive in the present.

We are learning, from Susan Campbell's book *Getting Real*, that the attachment to being right is the greatest impediment to getting closer to each other and closer to our shared Truth. Now we practice being real instead of being right.

Marriage is my second greatest teacher, right after motherhood. I suppose one could just say LOVE is my instructor in all things. I believe we are here to love. The most important thing I can do is to be the light of love that I am, inspiring others to do the same.

I have one word that guides me, and that word is "check." In my mind it stands for "Change my corner of the world through chiropractic, creativity and kindness." Every day I ask myself, "Have I made a difference today?" If I can answer "check!" it's a great day.

And do you know what I find? Almost every day of my life is a great day because almost every day I can answer YES. My little reminders help me to arrive in the "now."

Gems from Venus

- *You are unique, and that's good.* You don't have to look like or act like others; just be you. You are special; let it come through, and you will be happier. You cannot truly be anything other than yourself; you can suppress or you can experience it; I say be fully yourself.

- *You have something to bring that only you can bring to this world* – if you're hiding that part, the world loses.

- *Really explore the power of yes and no.* If you own your "no's," your "yeses" will be real. We are taught to say yes; reclaiming no makes yes more real.

- *Say yes to things that may push your edges.* Allow yourself to do this, even if these new ways don't fit into your family, community vision, or self-image. Try new things.

My family consisted of Mom, Dad and two older brothers, making me the youngest of three siblings. Both of my parents are deceased; Dad died at only fifty-nine, when I was eighteen. Mom died when I was forty.

My early memories were of simple fun. Our family had means enough to do getaways in Thousand Islands, and Wolfe Island on Lake Ontario – we took weekend trips boating and fishing. Those were wonderful family memories.

I consider myself a hearty person who likes snow, but I don't like living in it. Now that I'm out of New England, I miss the intensity of fall color changes, crocuses, and pussy willows of spring and in summer, fresh corn and green beans.

It was a wonderful place to be raised, with a strong sense of community. We all knew each other, they all knew our parents; teachers knew my older brothers.

It was fun being both the youngest and the only girl. And as the only granddaughter, I felt special. Because I lived in the country with brothers, and few other girls in the neighborhood, I had dolls, which became my best friends.

My parents separated when I was fifteen, a very tender time for me. My father was frail and an angry alcoholic, so I understood why my mother could no longer live with his disease.

My Chosen Career

My maternal grandmother had been a Bellevue graduate professional nurse, inspiring me by her stories. I loved to listen to her tell of her "cases." She worked until she was sixty-five.

I graduated from Russell Sage College in Troy, New York in 1970, starting as a foreign language major, since travel was and still is a passion of mine. My grandmother advised me not to become a nurse, that the work was "too hard." Surprisingly, as soon as she died, I changed my major to nursing. I think she would have been proud. At the time of writing this, I am still working as a registered nurse with a focus in Research Nursing. I still love nursing, and can't imagine a different career.

Some of my dearest friends still live back where we grew up. They know me inside and out, and we visit regularly. I continue to love to travel.

I landed in San Francisco after moving west from Boston in 1974, thinking I would spend only a year here. I was traveling with Russell, the man I married. We share a beautiful and talented daughter named Mesha.

The weather was so great here in California that we settled west. I am a settler; I love putting my roots in a home and growing it.

Most of my career work has been in the San Francisco Bay area.

I started working at the VA Medical Center in Palo Alto CA in 1974. After two years I transferred to the VA Medical Center in San Francisco. I enjoyed working with the veterans for another thirty years.

My elder brother and both grandfathers served in the military. I was afraid to serve far from home during Vietnam wartime, but I was happy to care for veterans who had served our nation.

Most of the work at the VA was with men, which was challenging. There was a lot of autonomy and mobility working in government service. It was helpful to me to have a bachelor's degree in nursing and then later earning a Master's degree in 1985.

My husband and I divorced when our daughter was three. I raised her with help from my life partner George, and with support of many dear and loving friends.

I worked full-time, retiring in 2004 after thirty-two years at the VA. Immediately after retiring, I was enjoying reading books, lunching with friends, entertaining and growing a rose garden. But, over time, I felt that the intellectual challenge was missing for me. It made me realize how much I really love science and nursing. I was fortunate to become employed as a per diem research nurse, at the University of California San Francisco.

I have enjoyed the challenge of working with dedicated clinicians on cutting-edge science, with special focus on metabolic, neurological, and oncological diseases.

It is amazing to me to work with patients with Type 1 diabetes, and to witness their progress as they undergo islet cell transplants, giving hope – after a lifetime – to become free of diabetes. It feels exhilarating to be able to work with patients brave enough to give it a try. They are inspiring.

On my days off, I love spending time with my family, playing with grandchildren, meeting with friends, of which I have a really large circle. But there is always room for more! I am involved with my church, which has provided me with wonderful supportive friends. I am on the Board of Directors with a ski club; and I regularly ride my bicycle and love to walk all over the city of San Francisco. I like to hike in the areas where I travel.

On Friendship

Friends have always been my teachers. The desire to connect, share, and exchange makes the world a better place.

As far as friendship goes, I'm very much like my mother, who had a large circle of friends from all classes and areas. She befriended kids, elders and everyone in between. She was an incredible magnet for drawing friends. I always remember her words: "To have a friend you must be a friend."

People extend themselves. You can tell when you want to be a friend with someone, there is something about them – maybe what they're doing, or how they are doing it. Friends enrich us; we feel more complete through friendship and support.

In rare instances, I've had to withdraw from people who pull me down, either because we've changed, or because my needs from that friend aren't being met. At times I don't have what this person needs, to meet her expectations.

No two friends are alike. I love connecting my friends, telling them about each other. I'm equally at ease with men as with women. I call my women friends my sisters, because I never had blood sisters. "I love them like brothers," I often say, because that's what I've known!

I feel that having such wonderful friends is one of my greatest blessings. I love to give them the gift of friendship, being part of their children's lives, and having a unique relationship with each person in the family.

It's easy for me to have friends. I would be lost without them. I am devastated when I lose a friend; each one holds such an important place for me.

The beauty of this life happens when we make the effort to connect with others. I always have a goal of meeting some new friends every year.

I have learned that if you want to see someone, to ask them something, or if you want more family history - get it now, while we can still think. Share it now with young family members. They will remember and appreciate it later.

My married daughter, Mesha, is now asking questions about our family history. My mother left notes about everything. I find that I am starting to do that, even putting notes on family historical items.

When a friend passes, I always remember the last time I was with that person. Even if I'm running out the door, I always take the time to run back and tell my loved ones I love them.

A Nurse Reflects on Death

My friend Jim, a ski buddy in his 70s, died last year. In his absence, I think of him, and try to be like him. I remember that it was his zeal that I most admired. I now carry part of the torch he had carried.

My partner George and I both joined the board of our ski directors when Jim died, serving in his honor. It was something we probably would not have done if he were still alive. It was a tribute, a simple way to honor someone who totally inspired us!

Regarding death, one thing I've learned from nursing, and also from losing my parents when I was young: death is going to happen to all of us. It is part of the life cycle, like birth, relationships, creaky joints and sore feet. We must cope with those things that come along –telling ourselves, "Hey, it could be worse."

When we're young, we fear death and we fear the pain. I have noted that when people are strong, having lived a full and joyful life, they are not resistant to death. When my mother was nearing death, I was amazed at how ready she was to go. She prayed to die. As she took my hand the last time I saw her, she looked me right in the eyes, and said, "Please pray too that I will die." I said I would pray that she would die in peace when it's her time. She died quietly in our family home three months later. My friends from childhood were with her in her final days.

I believe that people die the way they have lived. If you found joy in the simple things, if you did what you really wanted to do, and didn't look back at the "shoulda, coulda, wouldas," then you die in peace, with few regrets.

On Suffering

There is suffering. We all have some, emotional and physical. Today we have better care for those with physical suffering. But the emotional suffering persists. Each of us has to take care of that, every single day of our lives in our own ways, living the moments we are given. There are dark hours and dark days; the dreariness of winter brings that out in me.

I have learned to love autumn, though for years it was my least favorite time of year. To me, fall signifies a letting go of the warmth of summer, watching trees fade. My mother died in autumn, it left me sad at that time of the year. I now see it as a peaceful and pensive time, a time of coming home to myself.

We easily enjoy roses in bloom, but also endure bleakness of winter to truly appreciate the new buds of spring. I love being outside, in nature, enjoying sunlight, sunsets, and the shades of day in between, the music of the birds in morning, and the quiet of dusk as evening falls. I find my greatest hope in nature, seeing things that are alive, and the innocence of small children who love to have simple fun. Perhaps I don't let myself be quiet enough to truly feel the sorrow, as I so love the exhilaration.

We shouldn't fear sorrow, but I don't like to wallow in it. I don't like to stay in dark places for too long. When I have a dark day, I spend quiet time; I also am comfortable reaching out to others to help me. I have a few older friends, one who has been totally disabled in wheelchair with cerebral palsy since birth. When I feel down I visit her, and she pulls me out of it. She so alive and has so much left in terms of physical integrity, even with her many challenges.

I find a way to put myself in the presence of others; that helps me not feel sorry for myself. Sometimes I'll go for weeks without crying. When I do cry, I feel a total catharsis. My tears don't flow easily. Laughter flows more readily than tears.

A Daughter's Love

I have learned so much from my loving daughter, Mesha. She is a most creative soul, who helps to keep me strong in the present moment. Her life has been my greatest gift. She is my teacher. She has encouraged me to feel my emotions and to have a good "cry." She is my rock!

We've cried so many tears when young. In my teen years, I cried myself to sleep many nights, having to deal with alcoholic parents who argued. Now, as I've aged, tears that arise are mostly in the moment, not from the past as much. I am at peace and in love with life.

Friends ask how I coped with losing my parents at such a young age. I know I sure felt like a grown up when I turned forty! I had my two wonderful brothers to thank. They sustained me along with my dear friends when I lost my parents.

My friends became extended family, outpouring love. My daughter, at the tender age of ten when my mother passed, was so loving and encouraging. This love and support, along with the strong foundation and ideals both parents instilled in me, convinced me that I had what I needed to carry me through my adult life. I continue to feel very connected to the spirit of my father and mother.

Notes on the Future

The time is so right, with women today wanting to retain eternal youth by having face-lifts and enhancing every body part, to know that you can also consider another way to look at it: you are perfect just the way you are.

Please, young women; save yourself a lot of anguish. Learn as early as possible to accept yourself the way you are – with your natural beauty, strengths, and gifts. Accept your foibles.

Gems from Heather

- *You are unique, one of a kind. You are wonderful the way you are!*

- *Recognize and appreciate your gifts.* Capitalize by sharing them with the world.

- *If you think you can, you can!*

- *Be an activist* – stand up for what you believe in. But also pick your torches. No one can carry them all.

- *Do what you're passionate about, not what others want you to do. Be your own person.*

- *To your own self you have to be true.* Only you know your true self. Love yourself for that!

- *Go to sleep knowing you didn't harm someone that day.* Tell those you are sorry if you did hurt them. In so doing, you don't carry a heavy burden into the next day. This can be very freeing.

- *Learn from error;* quickly forgive your mistakes, which are human.

- *Move on;* let go of the past. Live in the present.

Part II:
Inspirations in Business and Life

Lynn Gates Keegan
Leader, Author, and Woman of Vision

"Women need to find mentors and role models,
To help them develop their own abilities and self-confidence."
~ Lynn Keegan

Lynn Keegan, RN, PhD, AHN-BC, FAAN is a leader in the ho-
listic health arena, and currently works as Director of Holistic

Nursing Consultants. She was President of the American Holistic Nurses Association when I first met her. At the time, I was a new member, and she seemed untouchable. Over time, getting to know each other, a strong connection grew. She has been a role model, trusted advisor, and friend. She and Barbara Dossey have worked on many exciting nursing projects together, some of which I was fortunate enough to collaborate with them on.

Lynn was elected as a Fellow of the American Academy of Nursing and is board certified as Advanced Holistic Nurse by the American Holistic Nurses Association. She is past president of the American Holistic Nurses Association and is on the board of many organizations and journals. She has delivered scores of presentations in numerous countries throughout the world and served as editor for a series of holistic nursing books by a major nursing publisher. She has been on the faculty of several prominent universities. In 1991 she received the Distinguished Alumnus Award from Cornell University - New York Hospital School of Nursing, and is a five-time recipient of the prestigious American Journal of Nursing Book of the Year Award.

Recognized as a world leader, Lynn models a quiet strength and dignity, a commitment to lighting the way for other women. At home, she is mother, grandmother, wife, and author. Lynn is a truly precious person, beloved by many. Between her children, grandchildren, Golden Room creations, holistic nursing endeavors, and writing, she is a woman on fire! Her grace and charm are rare, and welcome in today's hectic society. Her wisdom is a gift to our world. I honor her as a colleague - and as a dear friend.

Lynn's Story

I was born in the 1940s in a suburb of Washington, D.C. My parents divorced when my mother was pregnant with me, partly because she was pregnant with me. During my infancy, alone with only one suitcase, my mother boarded a train with me, and my older brother. We left a sophisticated, bustling, east coast city to encounter a dry, dusty, post-WWII Oklahoma. She hoped, and reached out for a new beginning.

We lived in a tiny apartment, in a converted larger home, right across the fence from the Osage Indian Reservation. It was two little red wagon blocks from the grocery store, where we walked every Saturday afternoon to purchase, then pull back home, a meager supply of mostly discounted, day old foods.

My mother worked two jobs so she could keep us. These were post-Great Depression days, before child-support or government welfare. My brother and I mostly lived at day care centers until we were old enough to begin school. During the summers we were put on trains and sent to foster families on farms either in Texas, Oklahoma, or Arkansas. Mother arranged these stays through people from work.

Some of the families we stayed with were kind, others less favorable. Sometimes we went to the same family, other times we were split up. It was on these remote, isolated, farms at the end of long, dusty, dirt roads, that I developed an affinity for the earth, and for the struggles of poor, rural people. I became one of them, learning to plant, tend, and harvest what we ate.

This rural living included gathering eggs, and watching with amazement when a chicken was beheaded for a special occasion Sunday dinner or when a hog was slaughtered to lay in the winter season of meat. I experienced the ravages of summer tornadoes and the huddling of our bodies, a little too close for comfort, in the earthen dug out storm shelter close by the out-house.

Eventually my mother remarried and when I was ten, she had a baby. This marked the occasion that I was no longer sent away. I was kept at home to care for the new infant.

When I was twelve, we all moved to a small town close to the coast in Texas, a place where my stepfather found work. In two years mother had another baby and shortly after that she became ill. My first nursing experience was at age 14, caring for my mother after surgery. By default, I also cared for the whole ward of post-operative patients at John Sealy, the then-charity hospital in Galveston, Texas. Since those days it has become a large teaching hospital, a branch of the University of Texas system.

For two days and nights I shuttled between the patients in the poorly staffed, old-fashioned women's ward, tending to what I considered to be helpless, suffering, very ill women during post-operative vomiting episodes. I helped with bed pans while the busy night nurse did her meds and treatments, appreciating my help. It was in the midst of all that need that I decided to become a real nurse.

During the balance of my high school years, I cared for the family: cooking, cleaning, and tending the younger children, as my mother was too ill to do so. I carefully plotted and planned, dreaming about how to escape south Texas, and begin a better life for myself elsewhere.

Nurturing a Dream

I had absolutely no money, and only mediocre grades, since my after-school life left me no time for homework or study. I joined the Candy Stripers at the local hospital and networked with the school nurse about how to go to college. She only knew about local diploma schools, but did help me to get me started on the path.

All I knew was that I wanted to be the best nurse possible. With the help of the county librarian, I began the exploration of how to accomplish that goal with no financial resources. From my library searches and writing for catalogues from all over the country it appeared that Cornell or Columbia, both in New York City, were the two best schools in the country and I prayed that one of them would accept me.

It turned out that both of them were five-year programs, each requiring two years of college first before the transfer to New York. The catalogues kept pouring in. My mission during the last two years of high school became developing an action plan. Desperate to escape from Texas, I didn't look locally. The cheapest college in the United States was Western State College of Colorado in Gunnison. It also had beautiful, mountain pictures in the catalogue. I applied and was accepted.

Then, like my mother years before me, I boarded a train, heading to new territory in search of a better life. For two years, in clean mountain air with good, belly-filling cafeteria food, while working my way through the first two years of college from age 18 to 20, I grew two inches, adding many pounds to my previous skeletal frame. I studied diligently to complete the requirements for admission to the second tier at Cornell: biology, zoology, chemistry and required liberal arts.

Cornell likely only accepted me because of wanting to add diversity due to my distant residence and my multi-year bombardment of letters and ongoing pleas for them to take me. Again, in the early 1960s, the train and one suitcase later found me arriving in the heart of midtown Manhattan. I'd finally made it to Cornell University—New York Hospital, School of Nursing. Six years after making the decision to become a nurse, my real program was starting.

Cornell Years

Babysitting jobs, student loans and scholarships sustained me during the first of the next three years. After completing my first year, I was eligible to take the New York State board exam to become a Licensed Practical Nurse. Working then as a LPN weekend and summer jobs, coupled with more student loans, got me through to graduation.

After five bone-crunching challenging, student years and two years of work as an LPN, I felt experienced. I was finally a graduate nurse, and as so, worked in medical surgical units for a year. The only problem was that there were many more things I wanted to make better than I could accomplish as a bedside nurse. I felt I had the knowledge, but the hierarchy declared that I needed more credentials.

Graduate School

I chose Loma Linda University in California for my master's degree, primarily because it was close to my man. We met while he too worked his way through medical school in New York. We married in California during his internship and my graduate school. He made $3,000 a year, while I lived off loans and a graduate school stipend. During weekends we stayed at his residence over someone's garage in San Diego; during the week I roomed with a couple of elderly sisters who lived close by campus.

At Loma Linda I was introduced to the Seventh Day Adventist spiritual approach to health care. We had resonance. It felt good to join the nurses singing hymns in the hallways to awaken patients each working morning; I also appreciated the fact that the surgeons prayed with the patients before going into surgery. The two years at Loma Linda further opened my spiritual channel to working with the sick.

More Changes

After years of a variety of clinical nursing positions, raising children, and moving from one locale to another, I went back to school and earned my PhD. From there I taught, was director of a graduate program, and worked in several educational settings.

It was during these middle years that I became engaged with and devoted much of my professional life to the American Holistic Nurses' Association. As I served in most of the leadership capacities, I worked to instill a sense of holism into all those I taught, wrote for, and developed.

It was during these years that Barbara Dossey and I worked together to write *Holistic Nursing: A Handbook for Practice* and traveled the world to speak and promote the subject. It gives me such a sense of accomplishment now to see holistic nursing embraced as the essence of nursing, as a part of who we all aim to become.

It was also during these middle years that I met and became inexorably intertwined with my dear friend, Karilee. Her light and joyful way of moving through the world was an inspiration. To this day, we still find times to sneak away together from the temporal world and take meaningful sanctuary retreats.

As the middle years slid into the mature season of life, I chose to leave the university to move to a remote, beautiful place in the Pacific Northwest. Within the past few years I have redirected my nursing focus by joining with another old friend and now co-author, to create new places for dying persons at the end of their lives. We call these comfort, skilled nursing locations Golden Rooms. Interested parties can learn about our efforts to spread the word about these new settings for death with dignity through our informative web site, www.GoldenRoomAdvocates.org.

Facing Obstacles

Like most people, I've had obstacles to overcome. For one thing, I had trouble in school, not only because I didn't have time to study at home, but also because I couldn't read. It was hard being called "stupid" when I tried my very best. For example in elementary school, I memorized all the spelling words and scored 100% every week, but then failed the final exam tests because I couldn't remember them for so long out of context. I simply couldn't read the printed word. It turned out that I was dyslexic.

Then, I must have had some neurological accident because suddenly – when I was 10 years old, lying on the top bunk bed looking at a book – all the jumbled words on a page in the book "Black Beauty" fell into place. Suddenly I could read. From that day on, I devoured books. I discovered a whole new, fascinating world. I escaped to new places and new ways of being. My friends were the characters in my books. The whole world opened for me.

During my junior high and high school years, I sought out and attended a church. When living in Oklahoma, I found a welcoming congregation downtown that my brother and I took a bus to. I felt peace and a sense of belonging there, continuing with that denomination through most of my life. However, my sense of spirituality overrides my sense of religion. I don't feel tied to any one church doctrine. I find strength in what I believe is my connection to the cosmos, and to all other sentient beings.

Basic Guiding Beliefs

One strong belief is that friends matter. I've always found and had good strong friendships with women. These friendships sustain me during times of crisis or trouble, and enliven me during good times.

Since being married my family has helped me overcome other obstacles. A supportive husband and good children and grandchildren help sustain my belief that all things are possible. I wish the same for all other women.

Prepare yourself so that you never have to depend on a man. This was one of the things my mother told me, and it remains good advice for women growing up today. I take this one step further: prepare yourself so that you never have to depend on anyone else – not a man, your family, nor the government. One of my favorite authors during my teen years was Ralph Waldo Emerson. His tenant and essays were on self-reliance. They made sense and appealed to me then; they still make for good reading.

My advice for women today: get educated. If you are young, map out a program of studies and stick to it. Pick a profession that will never go out of style. For me it was nursing. If you are mature and your children are out of the home, go back to school.

Education is essential; a degree is essential. The beauty of these times is that education is readily available through online courses, community college, and continuing education programs. Take advantage of it.

Develop a self-confident voice. Once you are educated and have the strength of experience, the next step is to overcome fear of speaking out. This took too many years for me, and still I am not as strong as I would like to be.

Women need to find mentors and role models, to help them develop their own abilities and self-confidence. I had the good fortune to both observe and be mentored by some strong, effective women, and I learned a great deal. When you are older and experienced, offer to serve as a mentor to younger women. An early, difficult life filled with challenges, prepared me for the world. After poverty and hard times, almost everything feels good after that. I am thrilled with the blessings of my life. Each day is a gift; I strive to use the time to the fullest and enjoy all the fruits of each day, from sunrise to sunset.

I would say women can improve the world, beginning at home. I like to think we have our greatest imprint on children during their first two years, and it is our own children that we have the most influence on, of all the people with whom we interact during our lifetime. Consequently I urge all women to put yourself in a position to be able to tenderly guide and care for your own children during those early years, whenever possible.

At the same time, it is important to not overindulge our children. In these past decades of plenty in America, many children have been the center of attention, thus coming to think of themselves as very special. This creates problems when they enter the adult, working world, expecting employers and others to think of them as special too. I think many young adults have been dissatisfied in the workplace because they expect their employers to better appreciate them, rather than to see their employers as someone to whom they should be grateful for offering them a job. I think this is directly related to their overindulgences, a lack of home discipline and rule-based childhood.

After doing the best job we can with our children at home,

women should use our natural nurturing and organizational skills to demonstrate our abilities in our jobs. Upon obtaining real world work experience, women can begin to influence others, i.e. when they see a wrong, work with others to figure out a way to turn it around. We can become work role models, offering new ideas in whatever surrounding they are working in. Some women can and have become politicians, corporate leaders, unit leaders, or organization leaders. These exceptional women demonstrate "how to" skills to others.

Women can influence others by writing and speaking. Wonderful women authors and speakers inspire others in meaningful ways.

Dreams

In considering my dreams for my great,-great -grandchildren, I wish that these children be born into a world of planetary peace. I hope today's wars, replete with weapons and identifying one another as the enemy, will be a thing of the past. I hope the only wars they hear about are in the history books.

I wish that these children can be born into a "green" world; one that is self-sustaining, using natural resources. I hope they learn early in life to recycle everything; that nothing is wasted and everything is reused and recycled.

I hope that some of their behaviors will evolve to a new norm: a blend of contemporary simplicity, meaning less possessions and consumption and a greener, more natural way of living. For example, in the winter they keep the heat low and wear warm clothes and sweaters, that in the summer they adapt to warm temperatures and wear natural fibers designed to keep them cool, that they lower the thermostats in the winter and raise them in the summer and save on abundant overuse of resources that we see today.

I hope they live in houses and work in buildings with windmills and solar panels and other new technological devices to better utilize resources. I hope living spaces and communities are better designed for more environmentally friendly living, less reliance on automobiles, and improved public transportation.

I hope there are more individual and community gardens so that people have fresher food to eat, and better appreciate where it comes from; the labor involved in bringing food from seed to the table.

Of course, I hope that my great, -great, -grandchildren live from a place of personal peace. I hope they develop a sense of spirituality, treat one another as they hope to be treated,

And I wish for them to come to believe, as I do, that our primary purpose on planet earth is to grow and develop our soul.

Lynn's Gems

- *Charity and education begin at home.* Therefore, do the best you can for your own family.

- *Strive to do the best job you can in your workplace.*

- *If you have ideas on how to improve things, speak out and, when appropriate, form a support group to help disseminate your opinion.*

- *Rise to the level where you feel most comfortable.*

- *When you have been there a while, and feel you have grown and made a difference, stretch up to the next level.* Achieving one plateau after another in life brings great personal satisfaction, and helps make the world a better place for yourself and others.

- *We are each here for a purpose;* so discover that purpose and move into meaning.

- *Remember to imagine and vision.* When you dream, dream big! For all things are possible.

On A Farm

Dad was in the military, so we moved constantly. I went to seventeen different schools and lived in fourteen homes by the time I graduated at age seventeen. With all the moving, our family was isolated. A military family, it was also full of abuse—emotional, physical and sexual. The thing that kept me from being totally miserable was spending summers on the South Georgia farm with my grandparents. I really think it saved my soul to go there. That was where I got to be special, where I learned to connect to nature and the earth and where I received love and attention just for being me. I learned things that made me feel capable.

I learned to hand tobacco, to pick cotton, to climb high on the tobacco barn roof to help regulate the airflow for curing the tobacco. I learned to pull watermelons, shell beans and butterbeans, pick blackberries and help my grandmother can tomatoes. I could scale and gut a fish, skin a rabbit, bake a pie from scratch, or cook a freshly killed chicken by the time I was in my teens. These skills helped me feel self-sufficient; many women even then never developed such skills.

In my 50s, I visited the farm again with my husband and adopted daughter. Early one morning, I grabbed a rowboat and went to the middle of the lake to fish. There, as I listened to the early morning sounds and watched the sun rise, I burst into tears. "This is where I found my Soul!" I sobbed. "This is what allowed me to make it." I think I would have been terrible mess otherwise.

Abuse and Nurturing

My dad was physically and emotionally abusive. He spanked me with electrical wires (he was an electrical engineer). Then he slapped me until I stopped crying, which he called "feeling sorry for yourself." He began sexually abusing me at twelve, telling me that my birth mother was a prostitute, so I had "the blood of a prostitute" in me. When my sister and I once looked up "intercourse" in the dictionary (I was thirteen), my father's comment was "you girls would probably lie down and make it easy for a man." I didn't know to what he was referring; but it made me feel terrible.

Our stepmother was also physically abusive. She pulled hair and punished us by insisting we keep our babysitting money in a jar, then deciding to punish us by assessing fines. Whenever there was a family money shortage, she inspected our rooms to make sure everything in our dressers and closets was perfectly aligned. Since it never was, she took away all of our money.

From the age of twelve, I stayed in debt, because she constantly took what little money I had. I babysat up to 6 days a week when I was in high school. Because my parents stopped paying tuition in my first semester of college, I started life in debt. The first time I was out of debt was at fifty-five, when I sold my house, and could finally pay off all my bills.

But I was smart, and I was lucky to have some wonderful experiences in school. In my fourth grade year, in 1949, my teacher Mrs. White had a genius for nurturing children's special talents. For me, every day after lunch, for more than half the year, she turned the class over to me for half an hour. I asked them what they wanted to hear about, then made up stories that I illustrated on the blackboard with chalk. Mrs. White recognized my talent for creative thinking and public speaking, something I didn't fully recognize until I became a professional speaker in 1984. Thank you, Mrs. White!

Europe

In 1953, my family moved to Germany and France with the military. That was also an amazing time. I learned another language, because my family lived with a German family that had a daughter, Angelika, just my age. I learned to ski in Bavaria, where I was also able to watch Olympic ski-jumping.

And when we were in Europe (while I was ten, eleven, and twelve), we traveled all over: Switzerland, Norway, Sweden, Denmark, the Netherlands. I saw and learned so much. Blocks and blocks of bombed out buildings were still present in Germany when we first arrived.

I also began to experience the helper side of myself while young, even though at the time it was quite puzzling. When I was eleven, we moved to Paris, France. A girl in my class who had cerebral palsy became my friend. She always had an aide with her. One day we went on field trip and my friend—without consulting me—told her aide that I would care for her. The aide left, and I was requested to feed her lunch. It was scary to me to feed her a hardboiled egg, because I thought she was going to bite me. The yolk fell in the dirt. But my friend only laughed. She was so happy to have some time to be "normal," which I understood only years later.

In Germany I had an unusual teacher Mr. Burdick, whom I loved. He was a genius at relating to kids on their level. Our class was filled with military children. We understood "rank." So Mr. Burdick organized our class like it was a military platoon, with colonels, majors, captains and privates. Bertie Herman was the colonel. It was his job to get class started each day, with everyone sitting at attention and ready to learn.

I was a captain. Mr. Burdick put me, and a boy captain, in charge of the "Remedial Reading Room." We had students coming from all over the US, at different levels of learning. One student named Rafael Gonzales transferred from Texas in early in 6th grade. Rafael could not spell nor write. He flunked every spelling test. We had a small room next door where Mr. Burdick set up a small table with paper and crayons and gave us captains strips of paper, on which we wrote the spelling words of the week in crayon. Then he taught us to have Rafael Gonzales trace the word with his finger, saying the word out loud as he completed the tracing. On my last day we had a spelling test. When Rafael Gonzales' name was called, he announced "100%!" I was so proud I cried.

Midyear, my father was transferred from Wiesbaden, Germany to Paris, France. Three days after our arrival in Paris, the Seine River flooded for the first time in many years. My family was living in a rented chateau in Ruiel Malmaison. The water rose to just below the first floor of our home. People were going up and down the street in rowboats. One heavy-set woman became frightened and turned a rowboat upside down, giving us a good laugh.

Madame and Messr. Trappier, our new neighbors, had their basement flooded. The many bottles of wine and champagne they had stored there floated up so they could be reached from the kitchen. The Trappiers invited our family over for champagne! At eleven, I sat and sipped champagne and ate champagne biscuits. My strict Methodist parents allowed us this indulgence because of the circumstances. What an incredible memory of my first hours living in Paris!

During our travels, we had many wonderful experiences. Switzerland made a huge impression on me. We stayed in an old castle and the innkeepers provided metal water bottles with crocheted covers to keep our feet warm. It was the day before Easter. They told us a story that during Lent, the church bells fly away. Then, on Easter, they fly back again and ring and ring to let everyone know of their return.

There we were, tucked into our warm eiderdown beds on Easter morning, high in the Swiss Alps, when the bells began to ring and ring. For hours, it seemed, they rang the joy of their return. Even though I didn't understand the religious significance, it was magical.

Back in the USA

We came back to the US when I was in the seventh grade. We went first to Georgia and stayed half a year with my grandparents. I had gone to school there when I was in first grade, and now here I was returning in the first half of seventh grade!

At that time, there had been little connection between rural Georgia and Europe, so everyone was thrilled to have us tell them what Germany and France had been like. Unaware of the speaking talent Mrs. White had recognized, I nonetheless accepted being sent from class to class to teach kids about Europe and "talk German." My sister and I became celebrities in this remote South Georgia town. It was the first time I enjoyed allowing myself to be seen, since I had told my stories in Mrs. White's class.

We stayed for a half year, then went to Hampton, Virginia, where my father was stationed at Langley Air Force Base. I was no longer with military kids or farm kids. Here, the children were the offspring of longshoremen, very different from what I had previously experienced. Those were some of the worst years of my life. My father started molesting me. I was also molested by my grandfather and two other men hired to work on our house. I believed there was "something about me" that had to do with the fact that I was "the daughter of a prostitute," as my father had told me. My grades slipped. My self-esteem plummeted. I didn't fit with anyone. I had only one or two friends.

In my fifties, I was looking at my report cards and finally realized that those tough years were directly related to being molested. I never told anyone what my father had done to me, nor did I talk with him. After he molested me, each time, he gave me a lecture, telling me it was "up to the woman to say 'no'" to a man. I was extremely confused. My father was paying special attention to me and it made me feel important; while at the same time, it was wrong; and I thought it was all my fault. Even now (age 69), thinking about it, I get an empty feeling in the pit of my stomach.

High School

In Hampton, Virginia, two junior high schools fed into Hampton High. I went to both of them, making the poorest grades I had ever made. As I started high school, I vowed to do better—and I did. I loved being in high school, though I didn't participate much. In three years, I attended only one school dance and one football game. My parents had my sister and me cleaning house twice a week, taking care of younger siblings, and babysitting.

I tried out for a play and was cast in the leading role. Clearly, they never expected me to do well in the auditions. I was stunned when my parents said I could not accept the part. All during my childhood, my sister and I were prohibited from dance, music, art, even comics. My parents said my birth mother was a prostitute and held the archaic belief that prostitution was "in the blood" and could be inherited! To help myself deal with this crazy thinking, I developed a sour joke -- I was the daughter of a prostitute yet my father was never married to one!

Ironically, my sister started teaching dance at Brown University, largely because she couldn't find a class she liked. Several years later, my sister, who had been banned from dancing and acting, became a dance and performance teacher!

It was in high school I discovered I could write. I wrote a story called "Dear God, Love Kevin," a series of letters purportedly written by a teenage boy as he described the atrocities of his father after the family got stranded deep in the forest. It embarrassed my father when the school literary magazine published it. I'm sure now it was my own early efforts to deal with my father's abusive behavior toward me.

Father

My dad was given TDY (temporary duty) to South Korea as I entered my senior year. He was gone for a year. As my sexual abuser, he felt he "owned" me. While he was gone, my stepmother sent us to cotillion dance lessons, allowed me to date and go to that one football game!

Dad never talked about his work. He had been frozen at the rank of Lt. Col. because during the custody case (for me and my sister), my birth mother revealed that, against wartime military rules, he had created codes and sent them to let my birth mother know where he was stationed. She sent evidence to the War Department, effectively ending his career. He blamed my sister and me for curtailing his career, often wondering aloud why he had sought custody of us. Once again, my father was punished for his indiscretions; yet it was my sister's and my fault.

We exchanged letters when I was forty. He told me my sister and I owed the rest of the family nearly $750,000 because of the loss of wages suffered when he was frozen in rank. I wrote him back and told him I'd be happy to pay my half, as soon as he reimbursed me with my share of the money he had been able to earn because I never reported him for his sexual misconduct with me. He didn't remember his indiscretions with me, even when I reviewed them in detail. His only question to me was "Are you trying to destroy my marriage?" I told him "no," but very frankly if his marriage was destroyed, I really didn't care; I felt speaking the truth was just as important.

By then I was ready for him. I used the "Broken Record" technique. Whenever he excused his past behavior, I repeatedly told him, "I was not too young to remember; I am not crazy; it did happen; you do need to take responsibility for your actions." After an hour of this, he repeated that he did not remember any of it. However, he did want me to know he never intended to hurt me and if he had hurt me, he apologized. I cried. I told him that was enough and thanked him.

As he was dying of cancer ten years later, I was not drawn to visit him. I followed my instincts, though, and called one day. He talked with me for half an hour, longer than with anyone else at that stage of his illness. I told him: "I want you to know that I forgive you for all that you have said or done that was painful – will you accept my forgiveness? And will you forgive me for any pain I caused you?" He said "yes." Then, I was able to say, "Thank you for being my father in this lifetime."

At his funeral, I was the only sibling not crying. My older sister whispered to me, "Will you stop being such a **** therapist and cry?" I replied, "I'm finished. I don't have any tears." I think most often our grief is about not having gotten finished with the person who dies. I'm glad I did.

Growing Pains

My parents spent my childhood trying to control me through money. In the middle of my first semester at the College of William and Mary, they stopped paying any tuition, and refused to back me up by signing a promissory note. Later, I discovered they did the same thing to my sister. We both earned our way through school—she got her bachelor's degree and teaching certificate; and I got my master's degree in social work.

It's no wonder I got married at nineteen. My young husband, who became a social worker and later an ordained minister, invited me to move across country with him. We packed everything we owned—including our two cats--into a commercial step van that had a top speed of 42 miles per hour, and drove cross-country, visiting every relative on his side and mine. We spent a week in Texas on his uncle's 8000-acre ranch, feasting on elk and venison, mending fences, and taking wild jeep rides on the caliche roads.

Mentoring

One of our professors had given us the name of friends in Seattle. Norma and Jim owned a houseboat dock with eleven houseboats. We moved into a small one-bedroom houseboat and stayed for five years. They turned out to be very precious years.

Norma, a social worker, became my mentor. I got into therapy at age twenty at her suggestion. She told me, "The sooner you work on terrible patterns, the easier to give up; the more you practice, the more ingrained."

Over the next eight years, I spent six and a half years in therapy, working out the pain and anger of the preceding twenty years. I am most grateful to Norma, who was so right about ending negative patterns as soon as possible!

Norma also took me under her wing clothes shopping, showing me how to pick clothes that looked good on me, having me show my purchases to Jim. He was an artist whose opinion I valued, so his approval helped me to begin to feel attractive, and bring up my basement-level self-esteem.

I could not see myself as I was. In her teens, my daughter found a photo of me in a two-piece bathing suit, lying on the houseboat deck and said, "Mom! You were foxy!" I've felt sad for me that I didn't know it at the time.

Marriage

My husband and I worked together to put ourselves through college. He was an orderly at King County Hospital while I was a secretary for the China Project in the University of Washington's Far Eastern Department. Working and taking courses at the University, I was having a very tough time figuring out what I wanted to do for a living.

I typed all my husband's graduate social work papers, which was easy for me as a 120 words per minute typist! I also began to notice that I found social work interesting. I got a BA in General Studies, with a Social Welfare focus.

There were so many things I learned to do during that time. My young husband and I took up snow skiing, backpacking, got ourselves a black labrador retriever, swam in Lake Union—right off our deck—and hosted numerous dinner parties in our little home. It was a healing and nurturing time for me.

One of the greatest discoveries for me was reading! As children, we were punished for reading for "pleasure." My husband encouraged me to read, something I did with a great hunger, reading for months.

That time was the first in my life where I found it was acceptable to just "be." Even with going to school and working, there was time to hang out with our mentors and neighbors and to enjoy the natural environment of the Pacific Northwest.

To make sure I really wanted to do social work, in 1966, BA in hand, I took a year-long job in President Johnson's "War on Poverty," working in a ghetto area Neighborhood House program. I liked it enough to apply to UW's School of Social Work. I was awarded a scholarship that covered full tuition and living expenses. I really threw myself into my studies, for the first time not having to work my way through school.

At the end of my first year, my husband, who had taken a commission in the Army in order to avoid being shipped out to Vietnam, received orders to move to South Carolina. My dilemma was whether to stay and complete school, or follow my husband. I resigned from the school. Then, three days before we left, the orders were changed. Instead, we moved to San Francisco!

In San Francisco, I found work at Traveler's Aid Society, helping people who got stranded in the city a way to get back home. My husband left the military and we had a baby girl. I applied to complete my Master's degree at the University of California at Berkeley, which initially told me no transfer students were being accepted. However, I wrote a powerful letter stating my case, and was selected as one of the four transfer students allowed to attend.

Standing Alone

By the time I began the program, my husband had decided to leave me and our year old child. Now I felt I had to complete the degree so I could support my daughter. I asked my estranged husband to help me financially, so I could finish my degree, arguing that I would be less of a burden to him as time went on. He worked hard that year, paying support and tuition. I ended up with a straight 'A' average for both my years of Master's degree work.

Through his therapy, he realized he was not ready to be father. I had been married eight years. Having come from a divorced family, I wanted my marriage to be a solid base for my child. I waited eight years to have her, yet my plans did not work out as I expected.

However, my husband leaving me helped me to grow. He and I consciously created our daughter, but after she was born he practically ignored her. He didn't even go in her room to look at her. He had a poor role model for a father, and didn't know how to behave.

My husband had begun working at the Family Therapy Institute in San Rafael, CA when he got out of the military. It was a highly respected program, so as part of my Master's degree program, I enrolled in the three levels of training, including advanced family therapy, with them. It was an intense program where the instructors and entire class watched each therapist conduct therapy sessions through a two-way mirror. Because I was training with therapists who had been in the field up to 30 years, and received much appreciation for my work, I found out I was good.

I got my license two months after graduating. People I had worked for wrote letters to satiS.F.y the state (something that could not be done now). It enabled me to start a private practice while I worked part-time at Children's Garden with rescued, abused and abandoned children. I supervised foster homes and did therapy with kids. I also had a two-year old, while I was doing this very demanding work – and I burned out. By then I had enough clients to do my own private practice. I have been in private practice since April 1972.

A man I met in an aikido class told me about the work of people who channel. One he told me about was a woman in her; a retired nurse who read auras and could tell about a person's past lives. I wanted to try this, so I made an appointment. She asked me to disrobe and put myself into a metal 55-gallon drum that had been cut in half to make a steam bath. This, she told me, was necessary to open my pores so she could read my aura.

As she started reading, this small woman with bony fingers said, "You should be a psychotherapist; you came here to help people. You came to this earth to be a psychotherapist." I said, "I am." She replied "Good, you're one of the few people on the face of the earth who had figured out what you're supposed to do."

I was so grateful to know I was doing my life's work. It gave me strength. Then I remembered that in college, everyone came to my room when they broke up to cry. They all knew something about me that I didn't yet know. Finally, by age 30, I knew I had found my place.

I did a lot of personal work, realizing that emotional things inside of me were getting in the way of how I functioned. I became determined to figure these things out. When my marriage dissolved, I began work on how to not be manipulated. Despite anger and feelings of abandonment, I knew I had to pull my life together and take care of my child. She helped me to stand up for myself. I saw that I had to get stronger so she would turn out okay. I got so good at being strong, that by the time my second child came, seven years later, my strength proved overwhelming. My son encouraged me to learn to soften that strength. That's one way my two children have taught me.

I was still not sure I was attractive to men and thus spent a year sleeping around with a large number of men. Then I said to myself "I know I'm attractive, I could have any man I want." Once I knew this, I stopped. Now that I knew I was attractive, what I really wanted was a relationship

Second Marriage

My daughter was four when I got involved with my second husband, whom I met in church. It turned out he had bipolar disorder, which later explained why he never even supported himself during the seven years we spent together. He was unwilling to get a job, even when I was pregnant. And because I was self-employed, I had to have enough money for the family to take the time to give birth!

After years of trying to "fix" things, I gave up. However, after I had ended our marriage by asking him to leave, one day I found myself sitting in my yard, facing the gate mumbling, "I'm gonna sit right here 'til he comes back through that gate and saves me."

It was the first time my marriage to Brian made sense to me. I see the Earth as a giant school, meaning everything offers us something to learn. Suddenly I realized I had never been properly taken care of. My birth mother had neglected me. My dad came home and saved me from her, but began abusing and molesting me—so he wasn't really my savior. I had been looking for a man to save me my whole life.

My first husband didn't save me because fatherhood scared him away. So I married my second husband. He had no chance of being able to support me, yet I held onto him seven years. That's what it took for me to learn my lesson: that NO MAN was going to be my "White Knight." The only person who was going to make my life work was me! It took a lot for me to get this message. That was a truly great gift.

Awakening Spirit

A "psychic astrologer" told me I had a talent for psychometry—

getting information about people by holding objects in my hands. Looking for a class that would help me to develop my talent, I found the Serenity Spiritualist Church. They didn't teach phenomenology there, but they did teach "spiritual development." I started attending and eventually joined the church.

The day I joined that church I cried the whole day. I had not realized how important spirituality was to me. When I joined the church, I felt like I had "come home." There, I started learning to see how things work in the universe. Teaching was done in classes, where participants were encouraged to stand up and ask questions. I was terrified, my voice breaking every time I tried to talk.

I had long ago forgotten about my grade school teacher, Mrs. White, who encouraged my speaking abilities. But we were encouraged to ask our questions, no matter how "dumb" we thought they were, so I did. Lots of students started thanking me for asking my questions, saying they were also afraid to ask them because they seemed "dumb."

I learned to follow my inner urgings. Eventually I left that church, joining with others who had left it, to meditate and continue to grow spiritually. For three years, our leader guided us and answered our questions, helping us to balance and tap into our own deep source of wisdom. I learned to put spiritual principles into practice. Eventually, I ventured to put those principles into my work as a therapist. I was following these principles when I came to know Karilee.

Today

Today I still have my private practice two days per week. I also do phone consultations, create and host my own Internet radio program, entitled "Full Power Living, which I began at the age of 60. Dedicated to "transforming our world through the power and mastery of human emotions," this show has allowed me to share my accumulated wisdom with millions around the world, keep in contact with some of the most forward-thinking people on the planet, and inspire others on their human journey."

This year, I've begun a new venture (at age 69) with "Raise Incredible Kids" (www.raiseincrediblekids.com). I am determined to help the world discover how to parent children so they remain the incredible individuals they are at the moment of birth, without the necessity to "find" themselves later in life. We're offering written materials, seminars and coaching, dedicated to helping people everywhere live the incredible, amazing lives they have the capability of living—and that they came to the earth to live.

Incredible kids, in my view, know how to learn from their mistakes, become self-directing, make great decisions, are conscious of creating their own reality, and stay largely immune to peer-pressure. Incredible Kids create incredible parents, too. I've learned that kids teach at least as much as they learn. In fact, that's the way things are set to work here on the earth. When we work with our children as partners in learning, we make the fastest and most amazing progress.

I'm writing, too. In addition to my published booklets that teach parents how to help their children learn about emotions (for example, *The ABCs of Anger: Building Emotional Foundations for Life*), and other books, CDs and classes I have developed and authored. I'm completing two books full of stories about the incredible experiences my own children had during their incredible childhoods.

I've got stories about the time my nine-year old son located a free rabbit and cage, and had it delivered to our home as my birthday present! Or when my thirteen-year old daughter spent a week in London on her own, staying with a family who had children her age, touring Winchester castle entirely on her own. At this writing, they are thirty-four and forty-two, each having incredible lives and raising some fantastic grandchildren.

I have a list of projects that will surely take me into my old age—when I reach 100 or more!

White Knight?

In 1998, I married my third husband. By then, I had lived alone for twenty years, had given away all my cookbooks, and was ready to do some really creative work. Then I met Bob. At that time, he had a child whose mother was possessive and angry that I was on the scene. Within a year of my marriage to Bob, she was diagnosed with pancreatic cancer. Her daughter, Robin, came to live with us, and never went back. Robin's mother died 4 months after her diagnosis. It turned out to be a very intense time. The same week our daughter moved in, my sisters' fiancée committed suicide.

I had thought my parenting days were over, yet suddenly there I was, raising a child again, as well as helping people I love deal with their emotions and loss. By mutual consent, I accomplished a stepparent adoption of Robin when she was 13. I strongly believed it was my job to help this incredible girl, who had been so closely held by her mom, out into the world.

She has now graduated from Reed College and administers the maternal health program "Jungle Mama" for the nonprofit organization, Pachamama.

Gaining Clarity

Around the time I adopted Robin, my own stepmother came through our area. She said, "I never adopted you – do you want to know why?" I had puzzled over this question for years. "I was afraid that your birth mother would come and take you away while your father was overseas in the war."

I said, "But when you adopt, someone else can't take you away." She said, " I was afraid it would break my heart." "But my dad wasn't overseas any more when you married him!" I protested, wondering where this would go. She looked me square in the eye and said, "Well, that's the reason," and promptly changed the subject. That was a huge learning for me – to see how scrambled her brain was, how fear ruled her life, and how my suffering at her hands wasn't about me – and never had been.

I thought that someone should have warned me that my stepmother wasn't going to be a really good mother. I had expectations that she should have been a good mother. But that was not in the cards. I thought how great it would be if we all could accept "the facts" of how things really are, rather than living on hope for years that others will learn to be different than they are.

But I've learned that we get to choose where we focus our attention. Wherever we focus our attention, that area will increase. This was HUGE for me. I had spent most of my years focusing on fear and negativity. Suddenly, I knew how poisonous that was, and I stopped. At the age of 50, I decided that even though my whole life had been based on fear, I no longer wanted to be fearful. Following the principle of "Pay attention, not to what you want to overcome, but to what you want to become," I decided to deal with any fear I felt by introducing its opposite, faith.

To help me, I developed the technique of asking myself, "If I had a written guarantee from God that everything would turn out okay, and I'll be all right, what would I focus on, what decisions would I make and what actions would I take?" Then I did those. It's been nearly twenty years; fear is no longer an issue for me.

I studied the work of other spiritual teachers, such as Lazaris at Concept Synergy. He said, "Love is love is love. It doesn't matter whether you focus that love on yourself or on others. What does matter is that you choose love above all else." As a therapist, I had spent my entire career teaching others to be loving. Now, I choose Love as the guiding principle of my life.

Changing Me

Over the years, I've been able to change so much. By developing an understanding of how people come to manipulate, I stopped my own manipulations and have been able to help countless others correct the course of their lives so they are happier and more fulfilling. I no longer "do" guilt, worry, or shame. Worry is a misuse of creative energy, guilt is a disguised form of anger, shame is what we develop when we think something is "wrong" with us. I now know there is nothing wrong with me!

For the nearly twenty years I was single, I believed I needed to be in a relationship. One day, I realized I was hoping somebody else would make me whole. But one of the principles I learned says, "What you have inside of you is what you attract from the outside." I decided then to create a life filled with the love I thought someone else might create for me. I began, for the first time ever, to be happy and full of love in my own life.

When I met Bob I didn't need a relationship. Of course, that's when it comes. You must be the person you want to find, living the life you would like for him to help you create. Then, he can walk into your life and fit right in.

The Future

Today's world is chaotic. There are many ways to help children feel safe, like getting them out into nature, where you can all experience "no mind." We humans need to be able to balance mind and "no mind." Plants are "no mind," a flower does not question whether it will be a flower.

My grandchildren are becoming the people they came to the earth to be. They will not have to "rediscover" themselves the way women of my generation have had to do. They have learned to focus on what they want to become, instead of being stuck in what they wanted to overcome. Their children will be able to live soul-filled lives from the very beginning.

One of the guests on my program was Dr. Janine Talty, author of *Indigo Awakening*. She says that many incredible children have painful early lives. It's her belief that this occurs in order to strengthen them to do the tasks they came here to do. I think this is true of the challenging start to my own life. I know I am strong; with my strength, I have accomplished great feats.

When I was forty-two, I taught a group of prerelease prisoners at San Quentin who thought I looked young. They assumed I'd had an easy life. I sat down and told them about my life. The story was painful for them, with many of them holding their bellies. I told them we all create our own lives; that when we don't learn the lessons as they're presented to us through our life experiences, those lessons don't go away. They keep repeating and repeating, each time becoming a tougher lesson.

I pointed out to them that the toughest lesson we have in our culture is to take a person's individual freedom by locking them up. I challenged them that they had not been heeding the lessons offered to them, asking whether they would commit to learning or return to prison. I shared my idea that it doesn't matter what you need to overcome, it just matters what you're going to do about it today. I encouraged them to keep focused on what they wanted to become, rather than what they want to overcome.

We need the bumps. No parent can be perfect, ever. The earth is designed to give us imperfect parents, so we have things to work on and learn. It doesn't matter how hard the bumps are, you still can get beyond them. That's what we have to remind each other of as women – enjoy the ride, bumps and all.

Kaye Henzerling
A Philosophical and Fun Realtor

*"In the Midwest where I grew up,
There were very narrow rules of behavior.
I wanted more!"*
~ Kaye Henzerling

*I first met Kaye through mutual friends who used her services
for a home purchase in our area. When it was our time to buy*

a house in the same county, Kaye showed me my dream house, the very first house we looked at; I purchased it and loved it. Not only did I just love being with Kaye, as I still do years later, but I always felt there was something so special about her. She is very wise, funny, and able to maneuver well through the stresses of life. She brings her wonderful humor into every situation she faces. To me, that makes her a Really Hot Mama.

If anyone could turn the stress of home buying and selling into a fun experience, it's Kaye, who continues to ride the up and down waves of the housing market for decades with a peaceful and wise heart. And still, when you look at her picture here, can you see that impish glow in her eyes? Knowing Kaye has lent lightness to my life that I love.

There is something magical about this woman; she seems to always be laughing, at least inside. I think Kaye genuinely loves people, loves life, and makes the most of it. She is inspirational in the way she lives her own life, maintaining a balance that keeps her enjoying it. If there was a way to encapsulate her strengths, I would. Sharing her philosophy is the best way I know to spread her wealth. I hope you enjoy her story, with words to inspire us all.

Kaye's Story

I have been a real estate broker for thirty-five years. I did many things before this work, including working in a rare book room of a bookstore after college. Later I taught high school for one miserable year, which gave me a very healthy respect for teachers and how good a job they do. Plus, I learned how shockingly underpaid they are!

Then I managed a small UPS substation, waitressed my way through college, and worked in a winery. Real estate is the one that stuck. My aunt and uncle were brokers in a small town. I saw that they were doing well, and it seemed interesting, I liked the idea of not being stuck in one place, and eventually having the possibility to be prosperous.

It was a people job. When we moved to Sonoma County in California, my skills didn't allow me to do much, so I tried real estate and I really enjoyed it. Every day I learn something and constantly meet different people. I get to see a lot of homes and to know folks I would never have met.

In my worldview, there are so many ways of being, some undesirable, but all a learning experience. I still learn something new every day. My work is interesting, challenging and never boring. I met Karilee that way, restless soul that she is! If it weren't for restless souls who like to move, I'd be out of business.

Freedom

From an early age, I wanted to be independent, to be free. I wanted not to have to do anything that I didn't want to do. I did not wish to be burdened by possessions. I wanted always to have choices, and not to be attached to worldly goods, money or power. To me, freedom was my most important possession. I felt it was crucial as a woman that I always have a means to support myself, no matter what.

As a teen in the 1960s, the example I got was from women I saw. The main thing I noticed about the women around me was that they were dependent, having to rely on men to support them. I later saw women being abandoned when they grew older. They were left with no choices and impoverished. Since I did grow up rather poor, I had no desire to ever be that poor again. I resolved young that I would learn to always take care of myself. I believed it would be great to have a partner, but I also knew that I wouldn't rely on that person, or anyone, to support me. It was a conscious choice to never put myself in that position.

I chose portable occupations, like being a waitress. To me, as a younger woman, there was great power in having that skill. I could move to a new city with no money, start work and make money the first day. Plus it gave me an ability to travel. I was blessed with a very good memory, so for me, waitressing was easy.

I wondered what else was out there, so when I launched into my career, I never returned. Though real estate is portable, I ended up in a county that I just love, so I have remained. I love to interact and possessed curiosity about different kinds of people. To me it was all part of the experience of getting to know the world and not staying in a narrow view of it.

I find it very gratifying that I have knowledge that is useful to people. I have the ability to help people make decisions based on what I've gathered over many years, enjoying my life.

Opening Wider Horizons

I have a terrible fear of being bored. When I was young I would read a lot, though I wanted to do more. I like to be out in the world, engaged with people. Real life has endless drama and fascination for me. I don't like creating drama in my own life, however. I enjoy it better as an observer.

Today, there is so much interesting neurological research being done. Scientists have now discovered that even in old age our brains form new neural pathways, helping to make aging so much more interesting. I think it's great that we don't have to feel like life is all over when we reach a certain age, that surely now we will start forgetting. The reality is that we can learn all the time, as long as we stay engaged.

Research has shown that when we age, especially if we're not still working, it pays to be active. Join groups that help you learn new skills. Discover new friendships while you continue to honor the older ones. Travel. Travel always provides new perspective.

Challenge yourself. Don't accept that you have learned all you will ever know, or it's all over. Now, at sixty-eight years old, I feel I have been incredibly fortunate. I've done things I wanted to do when I wanted to, and I didn't put anything off. I did a lot of traveling when younger. I am still interested now, but finding I need it less.

I've been incredibly lucky; it's been a wonderful life. There is truly nothing I feel I've missed or was afraid to do. People's tolerance for risk varies, and seems to be immutable. If you develop an aversion to taking risks when young, you will probably miss a lot, due to your fear. The image I held of myself was that I would hold my nose and jump. I had worthwhile experiences that reinforced my ability to take the next risk.

I can see why some folks don't take risks. Fortunately for me, I did not have that negative reinforcement. We would move, sometimes with no jobs, no money; yet I knew that if I could show up and work, I wouldn't starve. That really was a great liberator, knowing I could take big risks and maintain that sense that I'd survive.

I have seen evidence that overly protective parents may

cause risk aversion in their children. These limiting early experiences could influence the rest of the child's life. Some folks are more comfortable being in a known space and aren't attracted by the new, or the unknown. They feel more secure being in a safe space. They are not wrong, just a different kind of person than me.

Having some profession, or some sense that you can support yourself, is number one. My sister had a degree in social work. She had been a social worker before getting married and having kids. When she had her first child, she stopped working. Five years later, she had her second child. She ended up staying out of the work force for seventeen years. When her marriage went bad and her kids were ready to leave, she had to get a job. She didn't even have a resume. She was never able to get back to a decent level in her field. Her economic situation is precarious, and she's older than I am.

It pains us all when women we love don't have better opportunities at this time in our lives. It is easy to crash on someone's floor when we're young, we can travel around without much. It is not so easy when we're older.

Believing at an early age that I was capable of caring for myself, and that I could always count on myself to survive, made a huge difference. To me, being independent was a much more interesting way to live. In the Midwest where I grew up, there were very narrow rules of behavior. I wanted something totally different.

Exploring

First I went to Los Angeles with a group of friends. We drove from Chicago to LA in a hearse! I arrived with $80 for a summer. All our worldly goods were stashed in the hearse parked out on the street while we were staying with friends. One day we went outside and found that everything in the hearse had been stolen. I had no clothes, no money, nothing.

I got a waitress job, borrowing friend's clothes until I made some money. On this same trip I had first seen San Francisco and LA, both of which I adored. In my youth, by Midwest standards, I was kind of a freak. Yet, when I looked around in LA, I thought there was nothing I could do to make me stand out in a crowd; they were weirder than I was, by far. You could be unusual and wouldn't be constantly pressured to stay within acceptable realms of behavior, as it had been in the town where I had grown up. I found that I didn't die of starvation; it was fine, even with no clothes.

I was raised Catholic, and spent twelve years in Catholic School. I was rebellious of the rules, in the ways I dressed. I did party a bit, and was considered wild – that was not an acceptable trait in nice young women. There were always punishments for not following their very narrow rules of behavior.

There is often repudiation when people act differently, like today the way some feel that gay marriage is threatening to marriage.

To me, it's always been hard to accept that people must feel threatened by others who simply act differently. It is all fear. It was nice for me as a young person to get away from all the watching eyes – it was safer, emotionally.

Fear is a terrible thing - and religious intolerance is all about fear. "My God is not the same as your God." So what? So that creates fear, and fear creates intolerance. So many things in life that make people behave badly stem from fear. I wish everyone felt safer and more able to accept difference.

Women I Admire

Hillary Clinton is my ultimate survivor model. She is so disciplined, someone who became her own woman even under the shadow of a very charming flawed man. What she put up with in the public eye is awesome. I cannot imagine enduring what she endured. She is so strong and so bright, a role model to me. She was attacked by many powerful men as being a "bitch," but what she did was exactly what a powerful person would have to do in the stream she found herself swimming in.

I also love Barbara Boxer. As a leader, she is so articulate, so bright; she has a very broad view of life experience. To me she has been a terrific leader.

Empowered women live their life on their own terms. They manage to remain independent while being connected to the world. Whether rich or poor, just that ability to be engaged, yet to be self-sufficient at the same time, is a difficult and noble act, requiring care.

Travel

I remember one time, years ago, taking a trip with a friend to Asia. Our suitcases never showed up. We were in a small place without many shopping options, so we were washing and wearing the same clothing we had on for days. Day after day we began to acquire things that we needed. When we pretty much had acquired everything we had lost, our suitcases appeared, like a cosmic joke.

Traveling makes you learn to be resilient; you have to think on your feet and learn to fix it, whatever it is. I think traveling is very growth-producing for everyone. We need to get outside our country and see what is important to people in other parts of the world. Leaving our country gives a whole new viewpoint; things that we value most here are not valued elsewhere, which ends up helping us to understand another perspective. This is always valuable, especially for Americans.

When you travel, you see that people can live all kinds of ways. People need to recognize that it is all about choice. People make choices often based on our own emotional makeup. It is important not to devalue their choice, or to repudiate them. If a person truly loves her life, she won't need to put yours down.

If you truly love your life, you won't need to put others down. Each of us can learn to appreciate that there are so many ways to live; none is the right way.

Kaye's Gems:

- Today's life is so demanding. Men and women are expected to do way too much, making life feel like one huge burden. Everyone is so overbooked, running ragged, and feeling harassed. *We need to take time to tend our gardens, enjoy our friends, and laugh.*

- *Having a partner that shares your sense of humor and fun is huge.* Otherwise you can easily feel isolated. When I met my husband in college, a good friend told me that I laughed more with him than with anyone else. With a sense of humor you can get through anything - and later joke about it.

- *Remember to be tolerant enough of others to be able to love and enjoy them. But also keep that core of who you truly are and make sure you are not compromised so much to get along that you lose it.*

- *Figure out how to support yourself,* even with children, so you can always pay your way.

- You do have to compromise to live with someone or have a long friendship. Sometimes we have to put up with behavior we'd prefer not to have in our lives. Weigh how much you enjoy the person vs. how much they upset you. *If someone makes you crazy, walk away. Why drive yourself nuts?*

- *Avoid situations where you feel you're being emotionally poisoned.* If you have a bad boss or toxic client, leave, don't poison yourself, it's not worth it. If someone is cruel, abusive, or unreasonably demanding, fire him/her.

- If someone in your family is toxic, stay away. You may find you can be tolerant and loving, but may also need to push back. *Refuse to accept guilt; if you can't be guilt-tripped, you win.* Distance works great.

- *Having fun is very important.* Laughing with friends and lovers is very important. Try not to take things so seriously. "It's only money. F*** 'em if they can't take a joke."

- If you aren't happy with your life, what's the point? *Take a risk - even if you're afraid - and change your life.* There is nothing to lose because you're already unhappy. You may learn something new and go back to where you were, or go on an adventure and learn true joys of the journey.

Satia Healey
Simple Joyful Wisdom

*"Gratitude for what you have
– and humility for what you are given –
are the greatest gifts within us."*
~ Satia Healey

Rich and I both love learning about the healing arts and have spent decades exploring new ways to help people feel better.

Our extreme focus on healing, however, left us a bit in the dark concerning our money. I had always felt that I had an intuitive understanding of energy and that money is a form of energy, so I figured we'd be fine. Neither of us enjoys bookkeeping, accounting, or anything related to numbers. As long as we could pay the bills, we were good. During those younger years, with three small children, our focus was our family.

When the IRS decided to audit our books, we thought we were fine. After all, for years we had been paying a service to get us "audit ready" (at least that's what their tape says when they put you on hold). Imagine our surprise when we found out that our books were a total mess. I prayed for a kind, compassionate excellent bookkeeper. Along came Satia. From the moment we met, I knew we had been saved. I hope you enjoy learning about this unusual bookkeeper!

Satia's Story: Family and Early Life

Right from the start, I wanted to please. When I was born, the nurses used me as their "Demo Baby" to show new mothers how to care for their newborns. I still want to please, but now I make sure my people pleasing skills do not override my "comfort" level.

My dad adored me and tried not to favor me, but he did. I was a "chip off the 'ol block." I looked just like him and was even called "little Joe." My dad taught me gratitude for the simple things in life, and attitude toward achievement. He passed on a spirit of "embracing the challenge." He would say, "Kid, the only encouragement you need is to be told that you are not up for the job. Then, you go and prove 'em all wrong."

My dad was known as the "Ragin Cajun." He could accomplish anything he set out to do, but never quietly. He was responsible for the design of some very famous buildings in San Francisco. Later in life, he became an accomplished chef, dazzling friends and family alike.

Mom was dynamic, the polar opposite of a PTA mom. My sister and I loved and admired her. She was a dancer, had great legs, wore miniskirts and fashionable clothes and spent money like it was water. Once when I was in the 5th grade, my mom stopped into the classroom with her mini skirt, incredible legs and black curls. All the boys said: "That's your MOM?" I was a star for weeks.

My folks entertained a lot and their parties were over the top. They knew many fascinating people. We once had the band "The Bookends," who earlier that day opened for Creedence Clearwater, play at our house. It was the 1970s and there was lots of excess: booze, dirty dishes, and overnight guests.

My folks did not hide life from us. We saw what they saw. I remember seeing "R" rated movies that none of my friends were allowed to see. My mom would even keep me out of school for a "Movie and Fenton's Day" (the ice-cream palace). I knew we were not the "Beaver Cleaver" family and I was both thrilled and embarrassed. Kids want to be like everyone else, and clearly, we were not.

My folks played hard and loved hard. There was always drama in our household. Winter months were dominated by the Raiders games; if the Raiders won, life was joyous. Sundays were our family day and usually started out with donuts and the Sunday paper. Most every Sunday, we would all go to the movies, sneaking in our treats and RC Colas.

Life changed dramatically when my mom was diagnosed with lymphoma in 1973. I was eleven at the time. She died two years later, and our family life was never the same. My sister ran the entire household while mom was sick and never have I heard her complain.

My sister is amazing. She is a wordsmith English major and an incredibly inventive person. Growing up, she used to make my lunch in a brown paper bag. On the outside she would spend hours writing questions and puzzles for me to figure out. She was so good to me. She took me to all her parties and never acted embarrassed by me. She taught me to swim, to drive, to play liar's dice and everything in between. We both realize that we are blessed to have each other.

Lessons from College

It took me a while to figure out my career path. I was always a hard worker. I worked all through middle school and high school in a variety of jobs: yard maintenance, babysitting, amusement parks, dental assistant and of course, movie theaters. I always had a job and always had money. I learned at a very early age that stashing away money meant having security, stability, and power. Since my family always lived for the moment, there was never monetary peace in our house. I vowed to never live like that.

I went to college for my BS in speech pathology, only to discover that the only jobs available were in the school system, which did not appeal to me. While in college, I bought a funky trailer and a bit of land way out in the boonies. The water pipes were frozen, but the sun was out. So, I put on my boots and nothing else, gathering snow to melt for water. It was all so pristine and I realized I had all I needed. We have so much in the U.S. and tend to forget what matters most in life.

Once, my TV picture went out, but not the sound, so I was able to listen to the entire movie, ***Same Time Next Year.*** I then discovered that less really *is* more. I still play albums on my wonderful old turntable. I am not a very avid consumer and outside of recent medical discovery, I would not mind the "good old days" one bit.

I worked in restaurants while going to college. After graduation, I sort of fell into restaurant management. For the first year, I would somehow manage to tell every customer that this job was temporary while I was waiting to get into graduate school.

A New Path

After 10 years, I changed course and started a bookkeeping business. I realized that I could finally incorporate my innate people-pleasing skills with my sensible money-management skills and truly help people. Lack of financial responsibility brings shame, fear, and dependency. Fear can paralyze a person, so that he cannot even look at his finances. My job is to organize the accounts and gracefully educate people on how to confront their spending habits.

Many people have no idea how much they spend each month and are too embarrassed to question fees that banks and credit card companies charge. They do not have a clear idea of how they got into debt, nor of the tools of debt prevention.

In personal relationships, often one person controls the money, forcing the partner to ask for and account for each dollar spent. This dynamic can bring fear, shame and distrust. Once you guide someone into confronting and then budgeting their spending, the fear tends to evaporate. It is essential to know exactly what you owe and why, so that you have the knowledge to question and negotiate with creditors. Knowledge is power, and helping people manage money empowers them.

Whenever possible, I try to teach the tried-and-true, old-fashioned method of money management: consider wants versus needs; use primarily cash; use credit cards only when you can pay off the balance each month; and no ATM transactions. The banks developed the ATM for "our convenience" yet the overdraft and transaction fees generated are none too convenient.

Our society promotes overspending through clever advertising. One is made to feel that he is "less than" if he does not possess the latest gadget. Overspending is like any other addiction. At first you feel good, then you lose control, and then you feel shame. My goal is to get people to be consciously aware of each purchase they make and then teach them how to reward themselves for every dollar saved.

I am really grateful for the career path that I have chosen. As with most things in my life, I realize that I have been very lucky. I was born into an extraordinary family and had experiences that most kids don't have, both good and bad.

I have naturally appreciated the simple things in life. To this day, I still feel lucky when I spot a penny on the ground.

I moved to the perfect sized town with everything at my fingertips and a community spirit that is contagious. I am living large in a little life. Life is what you make it! So far, it has been a pretty wondrous ride.

Gems from Satia

- *It seems the more money one has, the more fear will disappear.* Rich people are not cheap. They simply analyze their spending carefully to ensure that they stay rich.

- *Making more money does not equate to having more money; spending less does.*

- *Personal control of responsible spending equals power.*

- *Happiness is an inside job and is teachable.*

- *Gratitude for what you have—and humility for what you are given—are the greatest gifts within us.*

- *We just need to learn how to look into ourselves, to be willing to see.*

- *It sure helps to have great guides to walk us through the challenges.*

Mary Shomon
Internet Empowerment, Awesome Advocate

"Whether I am successful is not is not based on
what others think of me."
~ Mary Shomon

We first heard of Mary's work when we began to write thyroid books. It turned out that those suffering from this common autoimmune condition already had a wonderful advocate.

Mary attended one of our east coast seminars, where we were able to see a master in action. With the mind of a scientist, heart of a mother, and voice of a Real Hot Mama, she is a force to be reckoned with. Since then, for well over a decade, we have regularly written articles for Mary's very popular website on thyroid disease. Together, we have teamed up to insist that the public deserves better thyroid care.

I wondered what it was that made Mary so persevering, so determined, and so succesS.F.ul. Her story says it all. Mary is a dynamic and brilliant woman, who has shown others what we are capable of being. What I most admire about her – and there is much to be admired – is her willingness to jump in, with both feet; to learn whatever she needs to learn, and to just do it. She gets more done than ten of me, and plenty of folks think I do a lot!

I am grateful to Mary on so many levels and wish her continued success and great joy in her life. She is a powerful inspiration.

As a Certified Holistic Nurse and a thyroid practitioner, I view Mary's work as a perfect complement to traditional medicine and with the utmost respect. Helping people to understand their bodies and advocate for their own health is a great service, allowing us all to learn how to restore balance in our bodies and in our lives.

Mary and I agree that we are each our own best healer. A doctor can help with diagnosis and treatment, but healing is up to us. As a nurse married to an MD, I can assure you there are some great doctors out there – and, sadly, there are some not so great ones. Take the time to consider your criteria and shop for your physicians. Mary helps her thyroid patients with a "Top Thyroid Docs" directory to help us locate great local physicians.

Mary Shomon is a fierce and brilliant patient advocate, who has taken the heat and come out strong. Another beautiful Real Hot Mama! It is an honor to feature her words.

Meet the Amazing Mary Shomon, Thyroid Patient Advocate

I grew up in Yonkers, outside New York City. It was quiet in the Irish-Italian Catholic neighborhood where I lived and went to Catholic schools as a child. My mother was an Irish- Catholic from New Jersey, while my father's family emigrated from Persia. My grandfather on the Middle Eastern side had to leave Persia after his parents were killed in horrific religious wars. At 17, he and his sister traveled across Russia by railroad during the beginnings of the Russian Revolution, later crossing the Pacific, then crossing America by train, and finally arriving at the East Coast, where they settled.

His journey impacted me. Here in America, people assume we are safe. Growing up in a family that had to flee from religious and ethnic persecution makes me appreciate America; appreciate its diversity and tolerance. I have also learned that it's often those who take action and control over their lives who survive in the end.

Early Influences

When I was young, I have to say, I was fairly nerdy and academically-oriented. I wore glasses and braces and got good grades. As a result, I was bullied in grade school, which gave me a harder shell. It also made me realize at a young age that other people are going to project their own issues on us and we have to really work hard not to take on their baggage and issues.

My mother had a strong influence on me. She was hard-working, smart and very successful at a young age, rising quickly in retail management to become director of Human Resources for a department store in her early 20s, before marrying. She returned to work when my younger brother was in grade school and was always successful at her jobs, while staying on top of our household, cooking, staying involved in politics and maintaining her friendships.

She was a tough cookie though – she had expectations – realistic, but firm – and I knew that it was my job to study, do the best I could in school, and toe the line around the house. At the same time, my paternal grandmother was also an influence. A very free spirit, born originally in Persia and coming to America as a young girl, Harriet was a character. Clad in cat's-eyes glasses, caftans, and dramatic makeup, she struck quite the figure. She was not a traditional grandmother. No cookies or knitting for her! Instead, she was out protesting at demonstrations, traveling or working, while at the same time keeping a somewhat traditional home for her husband, my grandfather.

My dad worked for American Airlines, so I was able to travel to a variety of more exotic locations when I was young, even though we were solidly middle class. I had visited Europe, traveled to many countries and wanted to get more involved in international events. So after grade school and high school, I attended college at Georgetown University in Washington D.C., studying International finance at the School of Foreign Service. Those were the Reagan years. I studied Latin American diplomacy and economics, went to Brazil, then Europe, and was fortunate to be exposed to many new parts of the world, and learn Spanish, Portugese and a smattering of Arabic.

Since I was a young girl, I always wanted to write and was a strong writer. In grade school, my fellow students went on a class trip. Many had never flown. Being a veteran flyer, I wrote an article for them called "what to expect on the plane" for my friends (I even attached an airsickness bag and sample boarding pass). It was a big hit. I think it was the start of my interest in writing information to empower and inform others.

Due to my travels, I developed a vision of myself as part of a large world. After college I moved to Texas, working in an ad agency, where I learned about advertising and PR. The agency was my boot camp for marketing advertising, PR, television, radio, video, print, and strategic planning.

After several years in Texas, I came back to D.C., working in advertising (Ikea was a key client). It was exciting - we were launching their stores in the US, but it had an international flavor. I stayed for a year, then left because I was learning about the vagaries of the work world, and realized that some organizations were poorly managed, including the agency where I worked. I would often oversee commercials being filmed. I'd stay up all night overseeing the shoots, and might end up an hour late in the morning after going home to grab a quick shower. When management yelled at me for being late – after an all-nighter for a client – I decided that was it, and quit.

In a business someone else owns, you're at the mercy of their whims. I needed to make a change. So in the mid-80s I went to work for a friend with a start-up computer networking business, earning half my previous salary. At that time, personal computers were new and we were setting up local area networks. I had learned word processing in college and thus became marketing director, and also providing software training for clients. It was one of those points in my life – and there have been several – where I felt I was sent in a certain direction, one that ultimately made a lot of sense in the bigger scheme.

On My Own

After several years working with my friend, I went out on my own as a freelance consultant, doing computer training, desktop publishing and creating brochures and catalogues for World Bank and various clients and agencies. I loved being on my own, doing my own thing.

One of my clients was a government contractor. I started their media and grassroots communications department. We built it into a 25-person department with millions of dollars in major government contracts. We did grassroots outreach using radio, television commercials and billboard campaigns. We worked for the Department of Health and Human Safety and the Labor Department, developing communication programs that we designed and implemented.

I also had an opportunity to pitch million dollar projects that had social value, which was especially rewarding, like the 1987-88 campaign to help immigrants understand their amnesty rights. We worked in print, radio, television, and created banners and posters in 14 languages for their neighborhoods, reaching them in temples, mosques, and community centers.

After a number of years, I found myself weary of the corporate environment. Too many meetings, too much business-speak; I was done writing "mission statements." I wanted to be back out on my own. I became an independent consultant in communications, advertising and writing, working with a large variety of clients.

Around that time, I also wrote my first book along with a cartoonist. A parody, it was titled *The Single Women's Guide to the Available Men of Washington.* Self-published, I launched it with a friend, on Valentine's Day, 1993. It was covered by over 200 newspapers, was on TV and MTV, and became a big success in Washington D.C. This led to many media interviews and the book became a local bestseller. This was before the Internet, so we did our PR by hand, sending the books and PR materials to reporters around the country, disguised as Valentines, to get their attention.

A New Role

Around the time the book came out, I met my future husband. That was also the time I was diagnosed with thyroid disease. I felt tired, was mildly depressed, and had hair falling out. I gained so much weight in the following two years that I had to keep letting my dress out before our wedding! I had asked my doctor for months to help me determine what was wrong. She finally checked my thyroid, and found I was hypothyroid.

At the time, I thought thyroid problems were only for old ladies and didn't even know where the thyroid gland was located in my body. I couldn't believe I had this! I am someone who needs to understand a situation, and then how to solve a problem. I did research at library, finding one small thyroid book. I was frustrated, not well, and felt something must be terribly wrong with me.

Then I got an AOL disk and I signed online for the first time. I stayed on for 30 hours, with barely a break -- I was absolutely smitten with the Internet. I found there was a thyroid support group online, which allowed me to learn so much more. By the end of this two-day crash course, I had created my own web page on AOL. It was a life-changing moment for me to get on Internet. I connected with other thyroid patients, and noticed that the same questions kept coming up.

I then created a "FAQ page" for thyroid issues on the Internet. In this manner, I could help those needing help. It was an early prototype for my work today. When I found Pubmed.com online, I could read scientific journals. I began to research. Around 1996, I found out about a service called "Mining Company" that allowed folks to create a topical-based website. I applied with the subject of "Thyroid." By early 1997, my site became one of the network's top health sites, with increasing traffic daily.

More Projects

As a thirty-four year old woman with Hashimoto's Thyroiditis, when I got pregnant, I worried. From what I had read, I thought I would have problems with getting pregnant, but it had been surprisingly easy. I was careful during my pregnancy, checking in regularly with doctors and being my own advocate for my thyroid condition. My daughter was born at the end of December 1997, healthy and happy. Working from home with her, doing PR and website work, was great.

My husband and I then co-authored *Scratching the Net: Websites for Cats,* a spoof on the Internet, supposedly written by cats. It was a lot of fun. I did all the graphics and it was published by a national publishing house.

I continued in freelance writing and PR work, getting more involved in the thyroid arena. 'Mining Company' became 'About.com' and was bought out by a magazine company, continuing to expand. This was during the big bubble at the end of the 1990s. My web traffic was increasing, but I was concerned my information wasn't reaching those people who weren't on the Internet. I felt I needed to write a book. I wrote a proposal for *Living Well with Hypothyroidism.* An agent shopped it and got publishers interested. This was my first health book, written 1999, published in 2000 and it really took off!

On A Roll

I then continued to write health books for consumers, based on research I was able to interpret from the medical literature and interviews with practitioners. Related books followed. *Living Well with Autoimmune Disease, Living Well with Graves' Disease and Hyperthyroidism, Living Well with Chronic Fatigue*

Syndrome and Fibromyalgia, Thyroid Hormone Breakthrough and *The Menopause Thyroid Solution.* In 2004, my *Thyroid Diet* book was on the *New York Times* Bestseller List for a couple of weeks and was Amazon.com Top Health website in 2004, as well as being a nominee for the prestigious Quill Award.

In 1997, I launched an email newsletter, *Sticking Out Our Necks,* which was also available by regular mail in a printed copy. I maintain a huge forum community, am active on social networks like Facebook and Twitter and receive hundreds of emails each week, keeping me very busy.

Since the late 1990s, I shifted solely into thyroid patient advocacy and health education, so great is the need. I was invited to be on faculty at the Open Center in New York City. Meanwhile, I started the adoption process of my son, who was born in Guatemala and came home to our family in July, 2005.

In these past years, I've been writing books and newsletters, doing my own publicity, with lots of television, radio and newspaper interviews, as well as PBS specials and other communications programs. Along the way, 'About.com' was bought by the *New York Times*, one of the most respected news organizations in the world.

My brother is a political consultant, a friend and colleague of Barack Obama. Back in 2004, Barack's book was on the bestseller list and he and I were joking back and forth by email about our respective books. Of course, his went on to stay on the bestseller list for more than a year! That was fun, before he became so well known. I had the pleasure of going trick-or-treating with Barack, Michelle and Malia Obama with my daughter, and former husband, years before Barack Obama came on the national scene.

Today

In the last few years, my husband and I made the decision to divorce, and so I've devoted a great deal of energy to ensuring that my children have a happy, healthy home life, and building a good relationship with my ex-husband. The divorce was inevitable – I had put my emotional needs on hold for so long, and realized that I did not want to grow old without a full, healthy, happy relationship with a partner.

My About.com site is still one of the top rated thyroid sites in the world. I have completed eleven books on hormones; and am still on faculty at the Open Center. I have been featured in and involved in producing two "Healthy Hormones" special on PBS stations nationwide. I am also working on a book with celebrity Gena Lee Nolin, a star of Baywatch, to promote greater thyroid awareness. She was voted one of the most beautiful women in the world. We will share Gena's story, including what it was like to be on Baywatch, with thyroid disease, struggling to fit into a skimpy swimsuit, putting in fifteen-hour days. Gena went undiagnosed for many years, and is now passionate about helping others. Like me, she hopes to change the stigma around thyroid disease.

I have co-founded a "Coalition for Better Thyroid Care," a group to help push for improved diagnosis and treatment. We are online at www.BetterThyroidCare.com complete with a downloadable guide to creating local support groups. We have also drafted a letter that people can send to their doctor, to find out in advance if he/she can treat our situation. I am very excited by the work of Dr. Kent Holthorf and his National Academy of Hypothyroidism, also hoping to make national impact. I continue to have a large following: 16000+ Facebook followers, 6000 on Twitter, where I am "Thyroidmary." I speak regularly with reporters on thyroid issues in the news.

Whatever Happened with Oprah and Thyroid?

Oprah has such an enormous opportunity to change the world, for millions of women. When she announced on air that she had been diagnosed with a thyroid condition, we all cheered. For years before she even announced her diagnosis, I had tried desperately to get crucial information to her that could help her to feel better, and to lose her excess weight for good.

Sadly, to date, I feel she has missed out on sharing helpful information about her condition and its treatment with her fans. This is tragic not only for Oprah, but also for the millions of women who have this condition, yet are told they are "fine" by their doctors.

I wanted to reach out to those millions of women who need this information, so they could be empowered with knowledge. It was incredibly frustrating, watching her skim over thyroid disease, bringing in known guest speakers who simply could not offer accurate, empowering information for the millions of women listeners who struggle with thyroid conditions. I know many excellent physicians Oprah could have consulted, well-trained MDs, RNs, DOs, NPs and PAs coming from leading universities. We could have knocked her socks off on this topic!

Thousands of professional practitioners across this great land – many female – would have readily jumped at the opportunity to share their perspective with Oprah, to help her to better understand the basics of her thyroid condition, and to get optimal help her on her path to wellness. But she didn't. She said she was cured of her thyroid problem, then retracted the good news, only to redirect her energy toward menopausal issues, ignoring the thyroid issue entirely.

Oprah had a once in a lifetime opportunity to dramatically change the course of women's health. But I don't count Oprah out – she is so powerful and creative and there may yet be another opportunity for her to make positive thyroid waves. For the sake of the millions of women who suffer unnecessarily, I hope so.

Gems from Mary

You need to decide what YOU think is right - *follow your instinct and intuition.* Menopause taught me to trust my gut. I had gotten very good at being in my head, instead of my heart. That intuitive sense is perhaps our most important skill, yet we are so quick to dismiss information received by feeling. Whenever I've ignored my gut, I've gone astray. It took me turning 50 to know I have good judgment; that I must listen to my heart and gut. Research cannot solve every problem. Intuition is ultimately as valuable as empirical data in making a decision.

It is very important to find some spiritual connection; whether through religion, mindfulness meditation, or conventional religious practice --- whatever works best for you. It is crucial to have this connection, with the understanding that it is not just what you do and accomplish, but also having an awareness of the world, a sense of responsibility and compassion for others. This also matters.

Be true to a higher purpose. Recognize some universal design, whether God's will or divine plan. Ask for inspiration, then listen for answers and respond to what you hear.

Remember that you are the pilot of your body. In today's health care environment, we are the pilots of our body. There is a strong tendency for patients to give up control to the medical establishment. We can't turn our health over to anyone else. We must be responsible for our own health.

Be seen! Make difficult changes when needed, so you can at least be true to yourself.

When it comes to our health care, women must take back control, be informed and empowered.

My motto: "When God knocks, answer the door."

Mary's popular thyroid website is www.thyroid-info.com.

Dorothea Hover Kramer, Ed.D, RN, D.CEP
Diplomate in Comprehensive Energy Psychology

"Rattle those cages, what do we have to lose?"
~ Dorothea Hover-Kramer

I met this next special woman while studying energy therapies as part of my involvement with the American Holistic Nurses Association (AHNA). She immediately struck me as having unique gifts and talents. Not only is she beautiful, now in her seventies, but she also seems to have vibrant, bounding energy. Her background in professional nursing was augmented by advanced studies in psychology leading to more than thirty years of private practice as a psychotherapist.

Her most stunning contribution to the health care world is her work in defining and validating the use of energy therapies as a complement to mainstream treatments. She is a founding elder of Healing Touch and more recently co-founded the Association for Comprehensive Energy Psychology (ACEP). In the 1990s, I spent a few years traveling, learning and working with her, and together we wrote a book on the use of energy therapies for psychotherapists (Energetic Approaches to Emotional Healing, Delmar/Cengage Press, 1997).

Her story is amazing, as a woman surviving great obstacles to become whole and healthy. Note how she sought guidance both from spiritual resources as well as from "angels without wings," to bring healing to others. Enjoy and be inspired!

Dorothea's Story

I grew up in Berlin, Germany, in the hard years during and after World War II. I was conceived at the start of the war, at approximately the time Hitler invaded Poland. My mother was filled with anxiety at that dangerous time, and I have no doubt her distress was communicated to me, before birth.

As the youngest child of five, I internalized much of the family's anxiety. My mother and father correctly saw the horrendous double-bind facing the German people. If Hitler won the war, with his plan for world dominion, an endless line of prison camps and further human persecution would ensue. No sensible person would want that. Yet, if the Allies were to win, the entire nation would go down with tremendous loss of life and, with it, the major cultural heritage of central Europe. Either way, we, the real people of the nation, would lose.

My father was an idealistic scientist who held some hope that Hitler would liberate the German people and end the war quickly, once it was evident that German troops were greatly out-distanced by the Allied forces of England, France, Russia, and the United States. Like all scientists then, he was required to support the government, because of its strong support for scientific work. Whenever possible, my father sent Jewish scientists he knew to conferences in other nations, so they could later bring their families to safety elsewhere.

My father's hopes for an early armistice were not realized, because Hitler insisted on pursuing the war to its most bitter end, right up to his suicide in Berlin bunkers, a few miles from our house. Before that, Hitler had admonished all of his still struggling troops to fight the Allies to their own deaths, or else be summarily executed by his loyalists.

From age three until I was five, life meant severe bombings and frequent visits to a basement shelter. In the last three months of the war, I hovered within "saturation bombing" day and night, in the Allies' final attempts to pulverize what was left of Hitler's megalomania and distorted visions. It ended up being the deadliest war on record for non-combatant civilians.

Developing Faith

The long nights, listening to bombs whistle by the houses in our quiet suburb, drove me to prayer. There wasn't much else to create a sense of hope, amidst the chaos and desperation. My father held a strong faith, while I learned to pray from weekly Sunday school classes.

Pastor Dietrich Bonhoeffer, the well-known man who was later martyred by the Nazis, told me stories about Jesus. I felt that Jesus and this kind pastor liked children, even a little black sheep like me. Most of the time, however, I felt my presence was a huge burden, to my mother, and to the adult siblings around me.

War's Toll

Tired and drawn from extreme stress, my mother died mid-April 1945, just before the end of the war. It was a tragic time for me and for my family. My personal tragedy was unquestionably exaggerated by the massive invasion of Berlin, bringing foreign, and very undisciplined, Russian troops. The Russian takeover of Berlin lasted for four months, until the Allied troops arrived in August. By then, Communist rule of East Germany had been established, with East Berlin as its capitol. The Allies, barely tolerated by Stalin's Communist regime, succeeded in holding onto their sectors of the city.

This marked the beginning of the Cold War between Soviet control and Western forces—a visible dividing point between American democratic ideals and Communist totalitarianism--- which finally came to a miraculous ending in 1988, with the destruction of the Berlin Wall and the eventual reunification of Germany.

Devastated by my mother's death, my father's disappearance (to another country, as we later learned), and the turmoil around me, I prayed a lot. I also asked my older sister, Lisel who was head of the household at just twenty, if I could get some help. I knew I needed more mothering than my sister alone could provide. Lisel absent-mindedly agreed.

Aunt Martha

In early May 1945, refugees were coming from Eastern Poland, the Slavic countries and the Eastern provinces of Germany. They were driven by the Russian soldiers, herded like cattle down the streets. I eagerly watched for someone who could help me. I noticed that a short, red-haired, somewhat stocky woman put her suitcase down near our garden gate. She looked hot and tired.

Feeling both hunger and hope, I went up to her and asked, "Do you know how to make potato pancakes?" No one had made me any for months. "Ja," she said while looking at me, a skinny, little shrimp, with wispy blond hair. I later discovered the lady spoke very little German, as she was from the East and spoke mostly Russian.

Encouraged by the answer, I asked the really important question, "Do you like children?" "Ja," she answered again and smiled. I ran to talk Lisel into bringing the lady inside the house.

Lisel liked her and also discovered that she had a background in the care of children. We needed to take in refugees anyway, since we had a large house with very little bombing damage, at a time when thousands of people were homeless, living on the streets. So it came about that the lady we called Aunt Martha cooked pancakes and ran the rag-tag household. She was a much-needed blessing to my shell-shocked family of Lisel, my brother who was my fifteen, and my other sister who was seven.

Aunt Martha also knew how to curse at Russian soldiers who came in and out of the house as they pleased and banged on our pianos. Even better, she had talents at bartering to get us food, because despite the presence of rationing cards, little food was available in any stores until the Allies arrived. We were fortunate to have a garden and Aunt Martha's indefatigable resources in utilizing the black market. Many Berliners simply starved in the summer of 1945.

Finding Aunt Martha was my first early experience in using intuition. I knew I needed more than what the musically-talented Lisel could provide. Attractive and quite grown up, Lisel had an established life of her own and was involved in theater. And though nearly every public building was bombed out, theater performances (a favorite source of German entertainment) continued in Berlin, so Lisel was able to maintain her work in theater, which helped to provide us with occasional extra rations.

My father, like many of the desirable German scientists, had been smuggled out of the country by the British Intelligence. Before he left, he was able to connect with my aunt (my mother's sister) and marry her the day before leaving for the US. She was then allowed to enter Berlin and helped the family to survive the bitter winter of 1946.

Even after the Allies arrived in the fall, my school didn't reopen due to our teacher's deaths and the lack of electricity. The post-war years continued to be devastating, as the remaining half of Berlin's four million citizens struggled to survive.

Handed a Gift

One day, a neighbor came and held out a doll, asking if I would like it. It was an American Raggedy Ann Doll that no one else in the neighborhood wanted. It had black skin. I eagerly reached out to accept the gift of the little rejected "orphan." I actually enjoyed having a black doll, which became the topic of lively conversations at the dinner table. I made up stories about how she was a Moorish princess with magic powers.

The following year, the same neighbor returned with several baby birds that had fallen out of a tree. I remember my new stepmother allowed me to keep them. I saved bread from every breakfast, and brought water to care for the little fledglings. I learned to enter their space quietly and gently, so they wouldn't get upset. I learned that my hands, and my focused attention, could make a difference. Later, when I had my own four lively children, I realized I could soothe them, with my hands and my intention, whenever they were upset or sick.

When the birds were upset, bright red and yellow came like a cloud from them. When I held my hands over them, they would calm down, and emit a cloud of light blue. After a week or so, I took them outside and they practiced flying until they could leave for the trees. I prayed they would find a good life.

This was an early experience in hands-on healing for me, a process I was to study in the 1970s and spend the majority of my life practicing and teaching.

Growing Intuition

We finally came to America and I had to work hard to keep up with school. We had landed in a small town in East Tennessee. There, as a repayment to the American government for their efforts in rescuing us from the devastating situation in Berlin, my father worked in the US Bureau of Mines. My Prussian stepmother was very strict, making my upbringing difficult with her and my father, both fifty years older than me.

I found it challenging to learn English and the very different American folkways. However, I graduated from an American high school and went into nursing with the idea of learning to help others, though I certainly had many problems of my own and suffered from post-traumatic stress disorder (PTSD).

I was interested in learning how nursing could be more humane, and more holistic, with an in-depth understanding of the human energy system. I recalled that in my childhood I had seen various colors around certain people. For example, when Aunt Martha got angry at my teenage brother, I saw red spikes flying off her head. I also remember seeing dingy olive green surrounding my alcoholic uncle. I shocked the family by refusing to kiss him, because of his awful color.

After graduating from nursing school, marrying and starting a very active family of four, I spent four years practicing public health nursing in Taiwan and Singapore in the early seventies, before returning to the States. There, I began to hear about Therapeutic Touch, a system of energy healing, taught to nurses at New York University by Dr. Dolores Krieger, Professor of Nursing. By then, I knew I wanted to do more with intuition, in my work as a counselor. I went to several Therapeutic Touch conferences, where Dr. Krieger and other well-known healers gave seminars.

Healing Myself

As a now twice-divorced single parent with four children, I became interested in my own healing process, longing to heal myself from the trauma of the war. I realized that many parts of me had not fully grown up, nor become integrated into a healthy adult. I simply had not learned what many Americans know from childhood on—how to be oneself, with confidence, and a sense of self-worth. Although I had a good dose of courage and a willingness to try new ideas, my personal struggles taught me that I needed to develop considerably more emotional intelligence.

I attended individual and group therapy where I lived in Florida. Over several years, I met some of the leaders in holistic healing and became part of a psychotherapy group as a relationship counselor. One therapist I came to revere as my spiritual mother spoke about the chakras; the human energy centers. Since childhood, I could sense and feel my own charkas - as an energetic reality. Now I felt guided to explore the human energy system more fully, building on what I could "see," and sense.

In the 1980s, I served ten years on the American Holistic Nurses Association (AHNA) leadership council. Among the many activities they sponsored that I coordinated as education director was a regional conference in Florida. The founder of a program that later became known as *Healing Touch,* a woman named Janet Mentgen, was one of the presenters. I could see lights coming off Janet's fingers, as the coughing patient on the table began to breathe more freely, regaining her health within ninety minutes. I then studied with Janet, helping her to design the *Healing Touch* program.

We made the program into a series of convenient weekend courses that could travel all over the nation, in conjunction with AHNA's contacts. When Janet was asked to write a textbook for practitioners by a major publisher, she pointed to me and said (with her well-known confidence), "You will write this book." "Good grief," I thought, "I really don't know how to write very well in English. Besides, energy-oriented approaches to healing require a whole new language."

In spite of my doubts however, I persisted and found an appealing, acceptable language for the work. I later authored two more textbooks and a book for the public, about *Healing Touch.* More than twenty years later, *Healing Touch* is a well-known, seminal healing program with thousands of certified practitioners, many more who have taken the first, basic class and millions of patients who have experienced this form of multi-dimensional healing.

Bold New Adventure

After ten years of teaching, I evolved beyond *Healing Touch*, believing that psychotherapists would also enjoy using energetic methods for their clients. With the help of a close psychologist colleague, Dr. David Gruder, I founded another organization, the Association for Comprehensive Energy Psychology (ACEP). The organization is open to mental health and allied healthcare practitioners, with more than 1,500 members, currently. We teach our certification program in major American cities as well as in many settings abroad. Our annual conferences feature some of the best-known presenters of leading edge therapies, like Jean Houston, Larry Dossey, Dan Siegel, Donna Eden, Joan Borysenko, and David Feinstein.

It has been an exciting journey, one in which I felt gently led, both by my spiritual guidance and by the many angels without wings, who've helped me to learn to successfully live by following my own path.

Celebrate Your Power!

Thirty years ago, I was a woman seeking to realize her own strengths. My traumatic childhood in Germany, along with the American influences that pressured women to be both seductive (like Marilyn Monroe) and be a nurturing wife and mother, led to much internal confusion. The divine feminine is now emerging in many beautiful forms.

Pleasing others is not our task as women—our work is to honor ourselves, moving forward, from a solid foundation, to assist others. As a grandmother and change-maker in my local and national communities, I would say to all younger women, "Own your divine nature, your place as a creator of social change."

Whether your community is large in a national, organizational way, or smaller within your immediate surroundings, I encourage every woman to celebrate her power, and to become involved. You may want to proceed in a step-by-step fashion. You may begin by asking important questions of your community such as, "Do the elected leaders respond to the will of the people, or to the dictates of a small minority? How are the elders cared for? Are the young people appreciated, and encouraged? Is any group forgotten or ignored because of ethnic background, belief, or sexual orientation?" As a woman who knows herself, you may want to join with others who have similar views and interests.

Remember to explore what's available – and what can change for the better —right where you live. Chances are you won't need to look far to find a cause worthy of your creativity and energy. Just ask around, "Who needs my help?"

I've become a rabble-rouser in my old age. I say rattle the cages of beliefs and limitations that may exist. Don't be polite. "Nice" is a four-letter word. What do you have to lose? For me, validation comes from knowing that there are professional communities, and groups of women across the world that care about the future. I find we can become quite independent, once we know there is a community out there should we need that, willing to help us to grow.

It's ultimately about building a network of support wherever you are. If you are not getting the experience of nurturing your soul, begin by creating a space for sharing your ideas. Surrounding us are catalysts for change, waiting to get involved. There are countless ways to be a change- maker; small is often better because you can see the beginning and watch it blossom.

Our idea with *Healing Touch* was that thousands of people, starting with nurses who wanted to know how to heal others, could also begin their own journey of 'whole person' healing. *Healing Touch* is now the only energy therapy that holds a strong national accreditation. ACEP grew from a small network of counselors, to a large resource for personal change and self-care.

Dreams for the Future

As for my dreams for my great grandchildren, I am hoping they will have a planet that has learned to live sustainably-- with fresh water, enough food, and good education for everyone. I hope they will thrive so they can give back to their communities. I hope humans can evolve beyond needing war. I know how devastating war is, both for its outright losses, and for survivors facing the reality of ongoing traumatic memories. No one truly wins in wars.

Even if a group wins a war, there is enormous work to clean up and heal afterward. Survival and recovery take time and continued, conscious effort. The devastation and defeat after the war I experienced was even worse than the bombings. We had to figure out where and how to live.

Currently, one third of the world population goes to bed hungry at night – that is not socially sustainable. I'm hoping my great-grandchildren will have figured out new and better ways to structure society, without its endless cycles of war, retribution, and recovery, then more war. Also new ways for addressing evil must be found, such as Hitler's insane notions.

Dr. Jean Houston keynoted our ACEP conference last year, speaking about "social geometry for the planet." She asked us to look at the real change agents – not politicians, because they tend to get stuck in their ideologies. Dr. Houston stated from her perspective of working around the world, "The people who are really changing the world are, for the most part, post-menopausal women. They are the ones who care about future generations. They don't need fame or recognition. Instead, they have courage to step forth and speak their truth."

A Grandmother's Plea

I have seven grandchildren. They are my mandate to facilitate change. I ask all women with a grandmotherly consciousness, the ones who care about future generations, to step forward and help to make needed changes.

We live in a global community. Even our cavemen ancestors had communities who worked together—to assist women in childbirth, to organize men for big hunts, to learn to grow food and domesticate animals. We *will* and *must* solve world problems in communities, working for directions greater and better than we presently have.

Women are learning to navigate complex relationships, as daughters, daughters-in-law, mothers-in-law, wives, and grandparents. Yet our most complex relationship is, of course, with ourselves.

Younger women struggling with their own identity issues could be helped greatly by women elders who have earned their wisdom. We're learning by Facebook, Skype, blogging, and whatever means exist, to reach out to others.

"We women have every reason to reach out and help each other --for our grandchildren and their grandchildren-- and to make the world a better place!"

"To the surprise of those who knew her, Dorothea died on January 15, 2013 of apparent heart attack, looking beautiful and vital as ever. Her contributions live on within us, and surely wherever she is."

Part III: Healing the World

Lynn Woolsey
United States Congresswoman

"Lucky me – my constituents, the people I work for, are
educated, antiwar, and pro-environment.
They care about the future, as well as caring about today."
~ Lynn Woolsey

There is a local woman whom I have been blessed to know for
decades. To me, she is the ultimate model of how women can

make a healthy positive difference. She has been our beloved Congresswoman from the 6th District in Northern California for a very long time. Her district includes all of Marin and most of Sonoma Counties. As Co-Chair of the Congressional Progressive Caucus, Congresswoman Woolsey has been a vocal and visible leader on progressive issues, particularly those dealing with children and families.

We first met Lynn Woolsey when our daughters were young. Shauna volunteered to make calls in a local election, dragging her younger sister along. Through this experience, they ended up volunteering for Lynn Woolsey. We began to attend her fundraisers, which were very unpretentious, often held in our local granaries or breweries in Petaluma, CA. We also have attended birthday gatherings held at her old Victorian home. We have enjoyed meeting her large family, of which she is clearly the proud matriarch.

A passionate and outspoken opponent of the Iraqi war, she has helped move public opinion against President Bush's failed Iraqi policy. She introduced the first resolution calling for our troops to be brought home and convened the first congressional hearing on military exit strategies, introducing H.R. 508, known as the 'Bring Our Troops Home and Sovereignty of Iraq Restoration Act.' The San Jose Mercury News called her "the unofficial matriarch of the [anti-war] movement in Congress."

Since her appointment in 1993, Congresswoman Woolsey has

used her seat on the Committee on Education and Labor to provide children and families the tools they need to realize the American Dream. She has been an advocate of special education and vocational education, fighting against job discrimination in Head Start and other federal programs. Congresswoman Woolsey also authored a 'School Breakfast Pilot Program' that was signed into law by President Clinton.

During her time in Congress, one of Congresswoman Woolsey's top priorities has been a legislative package called 'The Balancing Act' which aims to help parents manage the challenge of the balance between work and family. Among the 'Balancing Act' provisions are paid family leave, public universal pre-school, major investments in child care, universal school breakfast, benefits for part-time workers, and telecommuting incentives.

Having raised her family in California's North Bay and lived here for over 40 years, Congresswoman Woolsey understands the concerns and reflects the values of Sonoma and Marin County residents. She frequently said they are the most important voice she listens to. And she not only listens, she responds. Her Washington office alone receives and answers over three thousand letters, phone calls, and emails from constituents each week.

Congresswoman Woolsey's dedication to family issues and her belief in a strong social safety net are rooted in her personal history. As a young single mother struggling to raise three children by herself, she needed public assistance just to make ends meet, even though fully employed. This experience has helped to shape her commitment to family-friendly policies.

Lynn Woolsey continues to fight the good fight in Washington, completing her 10th term since 1992, representing our quirky northern California population in Congress. Lynn has stood proud for our west coast values and we honor her for it. She retired at the end of 2012

Thank you, Dear Lynn, for carrying our concerns back and forth to Congress, week after week. Thank you for representing us so clearly. Bless you, Lynn, a beautiful example of women in leadership!

My Evolution

I am known as "Lynn Woolsey, Congresswoman," though most people know me as Lynn Woolsey. I grew up in Seattle, where I had a traumatic childhood. For those of us with this kind of background, we fight hard to be normal. Years later, when I was in therapy, I had to learn not to be so normal. What matters for this book is when it all changed for me.

My first husband was diagnosed as manic-depressive. At that time, I had children one, three and five years old, and was the "perfect housewife," with Good Housekeeping magazine as my bible. However, it didn't work out for us to remain together. I had to go back to work, and couldn't depend on him for any help. In fact, his checks bounced, which ended up being *worse* than no help.

I realized later, when I became secure and remarried, that I had a rebirth at that time, around ages twenty-nine going into thirty. For the first time in my life, I got to be me. It was an epiphany and how I became *Lynn*. It was then I finally saw who I was. How feisty I was, and how I could survive and care for my three kids. I continued to build on that.

On Work

I had never intended to work. My husband had been a very successful, Montgomery Street security trader. I hadn't worked for years, besides raising my kids. I did some work out of the house, starting a foundation for cystic fibrosis.

The truth is, I was always energetic. When I knew I had to get a job, I went to downtown San Francisco, to an employment agency. There I took a test to be a secretary or administrative assistant. Unfortunately, I had always flunked tests because I'm a bad tester. I'm also bad at typing and shorthand. However, when I passed an intelligence test with "high" marks, the woman interviewer said to me, "I want to know about your life."

She asked why I was so sad. I told her I didn't want to go to work, that I never thought I would leave my children to work. Keep in mind, I graduated high school in 1955, then went to college. I wanted to raise my children and have a princess life. She was understanding and then sent me on a practice interview in San Francisco, telling me to make sure I told them I was happily married, on birth control and would not have any more children (they were allowed to ask then).

Then, to top it all off, I was to tell them I had childcare right across the street. I went to interview at a research firm handling high tech electronics, and sure enough, they asked all those questions. I lied. They gave me an intelligence test, which I did very well on. It wasn't hard for me at all. Then the personnel person introduced me to the head of engineering. So I went down and practiced interviewing with him.

First Jobs

The first job I interviewed for, the practice interview, I got. It was with Don Green, the father of modern telephony (who recently contributed to a magnificent green music center in our county). He developed Digital Telephone Systems. I became his human resource director. All this arose from one woman seeing something in me and going the extra mile.

Women – you have to support other women. And you don't have to lie anymore. If they ask certain questions, you have legal recourse. Even though I worked, I had to go on welfare. We lost our big house in Marin County and moved into a cottage. It didn't matter. My kids had shoes, clothes and food; and though childcare was difficult, we were together.

This was the beginning of the anti-Vietnam movement. I took my kids to attend protest marches, and was as involved as much as a single mom could possibly be. There was to be a large protest in the city on a weekday. The man I worked for was vice president of engineering, so I organized the engineering department to go to the Presidio and be part of the protest. Three hours later we returned. Don, my boss, later came to my desk saying, "It's a good that you're involved, and a leader…but no more emptying out my engineering department."

I stayed for ten years at Digital Telephone Systems in Marin. We started with 13 people, then ended up with over 800 employees. We built it, and it was a great company. We even had protection for sexual-orientation in the 1970s (possibly related to the fact that I was on the executive committee!). Then the company merged with a Silicon Valley company, and then a company from Florida bought our company.

The new owners took the execs out to lunch, telling us how wonderful the new company was. I asked them how many women were on their executive committee. There was a silence, as their president turned to his assistant and asked, "What did she say?" When it was explained to him what I wanted to know, his answer was: "Oh. Them. We have women in the company." They immediately undid our sexual-orientation rules, and it fast became clear they weren't going to put up with me, so I left and started my own human resources consulting firm.

One day, after I had been gone for six years from the company I helped to start, I was sitting at my desk when the phone rang. It was one of the managers who had remained at the company. This is what he said: "We just had a company meeting about personnel changes. And I said, those changes never would have happened if Lynn was here."

Moving Into Politics

Then I got an invitation to attend a meeting of the Sonoma County Commission on the Status of Women. I became chair during my second year there. I was then on the YWCA Board in Sonoma County, working with founders of the women's shelter. In my hometown of Petaluma, there was a land use issue over a huge development on the east side of town that didn't fit with any of the city plans. Someone came to me and asked if I would work with them to defeat the plan, since I was well-known as outspoken. Out of my new human resources offices, we started an initiative process to stop that plan. When it was over, it was the only issue on the ballot with the largest voter participation and opposition in the history of our state.

We stopped it. But then the city council announced our initiative was only good for a year. So I applied to be on the planning commission. After twice applying, getting three out of seven votes each time, I ran for city council instead, and won. That started my political career.

When Barbara Boxer decided to run for senate, she pulled active Democrats together, telling us that if any of us wanted to run for her Congressional seat, it was being re-configured. At the last minute, new boundaries put my town Petaluma smack in the center of the district. I threw my hat in very late. I was a spoiler for the men. But it was 1992, The Year of the Woman, and I won.

Welfare Mom Goes to Congress

In the last twenty years, I was elected to be a member of the House of Representatives ten times. All my efforts for the women's movement had paid off, because without the support of women in Sonoma and Marin counties, there would not have been a first campaign. After that, it was up to me to find my way in the Halls of Congress.

I begged for a seat on the Labor and Education committee, because I knew that was where I belonged. And I've never left. I later became the top Democrat (Chair or Ranking Member) on the Workforce Protections Subcommittee.

As a new member of Congress, you start at the bottom, as a freshman and as a woman. I was appalled at the sexism – I couldn't even admit to my constituents how hard it was. But I knew I had to earn my stripes. I knew I had fire in the belly, and that as a seasoned HR person I could hire great staff, which I did.

I learned the ropes and figured out how to be heard by joining other members who believe in the same issues, getting on their bandwagon, and helping them at first. It's theirs until they leave, so first you serve and help. I'm a good team player. If someone's doing a good job leading, I'm on that team helping. When there is a need, I step up and lead. I've proven myself this way.

Since Day One I have consistently voted against the war in Iraq. I have always been the voice that said, "I don't have to vote for the wrong things, and I don't have to go along to get along."

Growing Up in the Big House

I had to learn from others. Nancy Pelosi, who was emerging as our leader, would push "frosh" women up front on stage with her enormous generosity. She taught us to be gracious. She knew that she didn't have to be first; she pushed us forward, instead. I have learned a lot about statesmanship from Barbara Lee. She's a true leader and my partner in crime. Maxine Waters needed a partner too, so the three of us are a team. Barbara taught me that when people are opposed, you cannot shove your views down their throats, you have to be statesmanlike. And Maxine is a lesson in persistence. We called ourselves "the Triad."

I keep the energy momentum going, Lee is the stateswoman

and Waters is the outspoken one. It takes that kind of coalition to get things done. We have dinners at the Democratic Club, where we are seen planning and plotting. Those observing know something important is about to happen.

Don't think others will take care of your life, and your issues. This is critical for women leading - you must weigh in. This goes from your private life (who's caring for my kids) to caring how your kid's teacher is doing and whether the school needs support or change. Get involved. If you have an issue, get to be part of a group, don't just watch it go by. Participate!

Find the one or two issues, ideas or activities that will make a difference and get involved. We all have choices – all the way along. If the burden becomes the excuse, you're going to cut yourself short. It does have a lot to do with energy. I have more energy at 74 than most people on Earth. Positive energy is such a great gift. I am blessed in my life. One thing women tend to do is spread ourselves too thin. We can support and empower others – without having to do it all.

Gems from Lynn

- *Stick to your convictions, don't waiver.*

- *Be a good team player.*

- *Support other's issues.*

- *If no leadership exists, step up and bring others along.*

- *A real team player is as valuable as the leader.*

- *Don't hold back, get involved in what you have time/energy for.*

- *Don't think others will take care of your life and your issues.*

- *Participate, get involved!*

- *FOCUS* – don't do it all at once. I'm always going to support the issues that matter, but I know that I can't always be the front person.

Medea Benjamin
Dissent as Patriotism

"We felt that it was important for us as women to create a women-led response to all the male, testosterone-raging violence."
~ Medea Benjamin

When I was stationed at Walter Reed, caring for the US remains of the Vietnam War, I had an awakening. My first two years at the university were enjoyable. But then I started caring for wounded soldiers, washing stumps where legs and arms had been. With this up close exposure, I could no longer deny the realities of war. My roommate and best friend, Kerry, had quit, because she could no longer support the war machine. Though I stayed for another year, I was horribly conflicted. I went to Europe to study over the summer, and then returned to Walter Reed.

I returned to find that all of the students in the nursing class ahead of us had been sent to Vietnam. When I had enrolled, and asked about this, I was told that we wouldn't be sent there. I realized that with my high degree of sensitivity, I was not a good candidate for war. I had lived through early years of chaos, but did not seek war.

It takes guts to speak from the heart; courage to speak your truth to power. Here, I am honored to present the voice of a gutsy woman, Medea Benjamin, founder of Code Pink and Global Exchange. She has been described as "one of the high-profile leaders" of the peace movement (Los Angeles Times), and San Francisco Magazine named her on its list of the "Sixty Players Who Rule the Bay Area." She even ran for Congress on the Green Party ticket in 2000. For her current work, she is highly involved with informing citizens of our government's unauthorized use of drone warfare. You may be surprised to learn more about this!

Medea's Story

I grew up in Long Island, New York, in a typical suburban family. We were a somewhat practicing, Jewish family. I would say we were more cultural than religious Jews. My dad was a real estate agent and my mom was a stay-at-home mom. Neither of my parents was very interested in politics; they switched back and forth between voting for Democratic and Republican candidates. But they did teach me good social values, like caring about others and volunteering with groups working to address the issue of poverty in our community.

I was in high school during the Vietnam War and my sister's boyfriend was drafted. When he left, he was a sweet person, a football player. A few months after he was stationed in Vietnam, he sent my sister the ear of a Vietcong to wear as a souvenir. I was disgusted. It made me realize there was something horribly dehumanizing about war. I decided to get involved in anti-war activities.

At the time, Al Lowenstein was running for Congress on an anti-war ticket, so I campaigned for him. I also organized an anti-war group at my high school. We learned to play the guitar and sing great peace songs. We also took exciting excursions to New York City to meet other peace activists. I was editor of my school yearbook, which I managed to turn into an anti-war yearbook. I even turned the cover into a brick wall, with anti-war graffiti. When you opened it, there was a two-page American flag and instead of the stars, I put the word "Think." On the back, there was a picture of a baby crawling, with a photo of the Hiroshima bomb and messages against the Vietnam War.

People were upset and called my home phone complaining to the point that we had to change our number. At first the school refused to even distribute the yearbooks, but then caved in when we protested their holding our yearbook hostage.

Our advisor nearly got fired for it, even though we had kept what we were doing secret from him. After that, they changed the way they let students do the yearbook. I was fired up, yet inexperienced, I have learned along the way. I learned there were a lot of forces aligned in favor of war. That war took good kids, and turned them into crazed killers.

A True Education in Government

In high school, I was able to take some college level courses. One of my professors was from the Caribbean. He had been very active in his home country of Guyana, but had been forced to leave his homeland for political reasons. He became a big influence on me, giving me eye-opening books about colonialism and US policy over the years, and its negative impact on Africa, Latin America and the Caribbean. One of the first books was title, *How Europe Underdeveloped Africa,* and it had such an impact on me that I decided I wanted to travel around the world and learn about these issues firsthand.

I traveled, learned several languages, and ended up getting a job with the United Nations in Africa, where I spent many years working with malnourished children. I was appalled that there was so much food in the world, but such a mal-distribution of resources that children were dying (including in my arms) from malnutrition. There is nothing like having babies dying in your arms to convince you that something is profoundly wrong about the way we, as a global society, are distributing our resources.

I was especially appalled by all the money flowing into the arms trade, by all the wars I saw raging from Africa to Latin America, and how my own government was often on the wrong side, supporting repressive regimes instead of people's movements, and fueling the arms trade.

I spent time in Central America and was amazed to meet young people who knew more about my country's history and leaders than I did, since our policies had so impacted their lives. I began to learn how my government had helped to overthrow democratically elected leaders from Guatemala and Chile to Zaire and Iran. I became a passionate opponent to this kind of intervention.

I felt that one of the ways to stop wars — and prevent new ones — was to take people to the regions of conflict, so they could learn for themselves and then return home as "citizen diplomats."

Birthing New Organizations

I started a group called Global Exchange that has, for over twenty years now, been organizing what we call "people-to-people" travel opportunities, often to places where the U.S. government has an antagonistic relationship, such as Cuba, Iran or Venezuela. Over the years, we have created thousands of citizen diplomats who return to their communities to advocate for negotiations and non-violent ways of resolving conflicts.

Then my life really changed after the 9/11 attacks on the World Trade Center. When the Bush administration retaliated by invading Afghanistan, I went to Afghanistan and found civilians being killed or displaced by our so-called "smart bombs." I came back from that trip very disturbed, but discovered that the drumbeat had already started for launching another war; this time in Iraq. During that time, I was in a retreat organized for women environmentalists. We started talking about the imminent war and the Bush administration's color-coding of "threats" — it's 'code orange' and 'code red.' Someone said in jest that we should create a 'code pink' and so we did.

We felt that it was important for us as women to create a women-led response to all the male, testosterone-raging violence; violence we saw from George Bush, to Osama bin Laden, to Saddam Hussein. We held a few events in Washington. We honestly didn't mean to create a new organization, since we all had our hands full with other work, but it took on a life of its own and before we knew it, CODEPINK had grown to 200,000 people, with about 300 local groups.

Once President Obama got elected, many people left the peace movement, including CODEPINK, thinking Obama would get us out of the wars. But President Obama, who came into office as a peace candidate, increased the troops in Afghanistan and launched secretive drone attacks in Pakistan, Yemen and Somalia that have killed thousands of people, including many women and children. That is why I wrote a new book, titled *Drone Warfare*. I am traveling around the U.S., mobilizing citizens against this new wave of killing by remote control.

I hope we can change public opinion, to pressure the Obama administration to have a foreign policy in line with what most Americans believe and want. We need a foreign policy that allows us to stop creating new enemies overseas, and instead allows us to put our resources into rebuilding our own nation, finding effective ways to address the real crisis of global warming.

Lessons Learned

I've learned that the tendency to continue making war is greater than the power of an individual in office. I've learned that if we want to stop war, we have to build a strong movement independent of political parties. I also learned that we have to link the issue of militarism to the larger economic issues, and to show people that we will never have the funds we need for education, healthcare and other critical needs if we continue to spend so much money on the military.

Another hard lesson for me was learning that no matter how successfully we mobilize — like the massive anti-war demonstrations we organized around the world on February 15, 2003 to stop the invasion of Iraq — sometimes our elected officials are deaf, dumb and blind. Sometimes they refuse to hear the cries of the people against war. It seems war is the easy path for them to take. They want to show themselves to be tough guys. It's a macho thing, where negotiation is a "wussy" thing to do.

I have realized over the years that the peacemakers, those who struggle to keep our country from invading other countries, are usually belittled. Meanwhile those who fight in wars, including unjust wars, as in Vietnam or Iraq, are considered heroes. "Thanks for your service" is a constant refrain, as if military service is the only kind of service that is valued. Trying to bring in a voice of compassion or caring or peace, you're often treated as a crazy person — even downright Un-American – and marginalized. I've had lots of hate mail over the years and many death threats. I've gone to jail many times for engaging in acts of civil disobedience.

It can be demoralizing and exhausting, especially when our government and media ignore our efforts. I have always tried to keep a "glass-half-full" attitude and to remember that waging peace is a lifetime commitment. I think of my peasant friends in Central America who work so hard to survive on a couple of dollars a day. Who don't have the luxury of being demoralized. I also remind myself of the terrible suffering that others throughout history have endured in their fights for justice. People like Nelson Mandela who spent 27 years in prison for what he believes. My sacrifices have been nothing compared to that!

Gems from Medea

- *Go with your heart.* It might lead you on different paths than you had planned. I wanted to work for the US government, in Foreign Service. Then I saw that my government has policies I don't believe in. So I tried to be a journalist, but as a journalist, I wasn't able to make changes. I was only supposed to report it. I wanted to make change happen, so I became an activist.

- *Always follow where your heart leads you.* It might not -- and probably won't -- be the way to make the most money and at times you won't be pleasing people (like your family). You may have to go on a different path, but you will be fulfilled by the exciting work you do and by the passionate, caring people you get to work with. That's worth more than money can buy.

- *Take risks!* Life is full of uncertainty. Life is ephemeral. Life is short. Make the most of the time you have. Swim in the deep sea of life. Dive into new opportunities. Let the beauty of discovery wash over you every day.

- *Free yourself from fear* and the world will open up to you, with all its joy and wonder.

Janet Di Santo, MFT
Transforming From a Dysfunctional Family of Origin To Personal Healing and Service

*"What I was doing was breaking a tribal law.
It was a bold thing to do."*
~ Jan Di Santo

I first met Jan Di Santo when we both attended a parents' introduction to a public school in Mill Valley CA, where we once lived. With her crystal necklace and trim style, I felt we would be friends. Over the years, our kids were in various classes together. Jan and her psychiatrist husband, Peter, have lovely kids, and I've enjoyed watching them mature. We've all matured over all these years.

Jan was a nurse by training, but her chosen field has been to work as a therapist. This has also been my work, so we've always had much to share, as did our medical husbands. And Jan and her husband have been loyal participants in an ongoing river gathering we hold every summer.

Fascinating to me, Jan and I have similar backgrounds. We were both second children in a big household, were responsible for caring for our siblings, and both had a mother that raged. We also both received our master's degree in psychiatric nursing through an NIMH Grant. We traveled very similar roads.

In her own delightful way, Jan remains a beacon of light in the Marin county community, successful in her work and personal life. She maintains a lovely home and garden, part way up on our beloved mountain, Mt. Tamalpais. I want you to hear her words, for while she wishes to maintain a certain comfortable degree of anonymity; she also would like to share her wisdom. She is a beautiful model of an actualized woman, living a full rich life.

Jan's Story

I was born in Detroit, Michigan. I grew up in a nice suburb called Grosse Pointe. I was the second oldest of seven children, the last born when I was in my first year of college. In my younger years, it felt like there were two tracks: active/creative play and dysfunctional family. I was very creative, as was my sister, who was one year older.

Our best friend, now a therapist in San Diego, lived three doors down the block. We lived next to a wooded area, which provided a rich base for our imaginative play which, fortunately, my parents had the wisdom to encourage. The three of us played together often.

The friendship and creativity was great --- we made spook houses, did art projects, had bake sales, wrote and put on plays and seasonal pageants. This was a wonderful part of my childhood.

Family Challenges

The difficult part was that my family became increasingly dysfunctional as time went on. Mother had a mood disorder, which eventually turned into bipolar illness. Every moment of every day, you never knew if you were going to get the happy or angry mother. I grew up in a very unsafe container, where I learned I could never completely trust my environment. It affected my ability to fully put myself out there in the world, fearing I might get attacked like I did at home.

My mother had rage attacks. I got yelled at less because I was one of the "good children" trying to keep things under control. But even if I was not the target of the abuse, to witness and experience the verbal or physical violence of it affected me deeply. As a way to try to control her mood and give her less to be upset about, I became very helpful. I began doing dishes at five years old. I remember surprising her when she was putting my siblings down to sleep. I had done the dishes and it made her so happy.

So I continued to try and keep her happy. The older I got, the more I took on. I was incredibly competent at very young age, but I was ultimately exploited for my helpfulness. I ended up losing my adolescence. While others were engaged in sports or other after school activities or hanging out with friends, I was coming home every day, taking care of my siblings, and doing chores.

My desire to help people was part of my soul path, and I was rewarded for it in my family of origin. With this imprint of taking care of people, when it came to picking a career, I first went into nursing, then psychotherapy.

Reflections on my Life

Looking back, I wasn't very nurtured in my family of origin, nor did I get much positive mirroring. Today my mother feels her biggest mistake was in not being affectionate. She's not yet able to acknowledge how angry she was, nor how it hurt us. In the past six or seven years, deeper into her eighties and in a wheelchair, she has had nothing but time on her hands to sit and reflect on her life. She is dependent on caregivers, so she now has to take the medication she always so desperately needed, but fought, earlier in her life.

As a result, she is more balanced and emotionally regulated, and it is possible to have a more functional relationship with her. Consequently, I am more engaged with her. She has learned to be loving, validating and supportive with me and my siblings. I no longer have to protect myself so heavily against her.

My Story Continues

Around age ten, I felt depressed at times; it got worse in adolescence. I didn't have anyone to talk to. My father worked a lot. He was a realtor, came home for dinner, ate, then left to show houses. He also worked weekends. His lack of availability left mother shouldering a lot, giving me even more reason for me to help her. Their relationship was neither close nor supportive.

The teen years were not great for me. I was not happy, nor feeling supported or connected. I did well in school, which gave me positive self-esteem. That became my life: doing well in school, helping mother. I did have friends, which was a godsend, but I often felt an undercurrent of depression, as well. I did not feel there was someone I could be safe with or nurtured. I wasn't being fed emotionally. I think this is what later attracted me to becoming a therapist.

Mother had her first manic episode when I was in college, though she denied there was anything wrong. It was then that I began to realize how dysfunctional my family was. When I heard about the concept of family therapy, it became my mission to become a family therapist, which I did accomplish. Somewhere deep inside me, I knew I had to understand the family I was born into; this seemed like the path to do this work.

I also pursued personal therapy while a junior in college, around the time when mother was having her first manic episode. It seemed at first that she was very, very depressed. I had come home from school for the holidays and she was terribly down. When I left, she slipped into a manic state. She was angry, talking all the time, not sleeping. It was of concern, because my brother was seven, my sister was six, and the youngest was only two.

It wasn't pretty. We were all trying to figure out what was going on, but I was five hours away in college and my parents weren't getting along, which made communication difficult. On top of all that, she refused treatment. I struggled with the pain of this throughout college and my adult years. One of my main concerns was for my younger siblings, who had to live with her. I agonized and obsessed over what to do, but knew there was nothing I could do. My mother was not only bipolar, but also psychotically paranoid. Her own mother died when she was born, so she had never had mothering or a secure attachment bond with a caregiver. This contributed to her paranoia.

For the next thirty plus years, she was on and off medications, in and out of mental hospitals and treatment. My father was committed to her care, but she became paranoid about him and remains so today. They eventually divorced. In her mind, there was nothing wrong with her, yet there were awful scenes where the police would have to take her away and she would fight it. It was confusing for my younger siblings.

Breaking the Rule

The family rule was 'don't talk.' Our family rules prevented me from telling the truth to the little ones in our family, putting them in a position that they would have to choose between what I was telling them and what mother said about the reality being played out. There would have been an ugly backlash had I gone against her.

Finally when they were out of the house, I spoke with them. They were relieved to know the truth, which was that mom had bipolar illness, which was responsible for her behavior. My one sister burst into tears and they were all relieved to know what had been going on. There had always been a lot of chaos and drama, with so many things not making sense. This put things into a new perspective for them and helped them start to heal.

Having to Not Communicate

In my adult years, trying to figure out how to have a relationship with my mother was incredibly painful. When I had my own children, I couldn't deal with her calling, ranting and raging on the phone. It disturbed the peacefulness of the environment I had created for my children. Consequently, I told her I couldn't have contact with her until she was in a stable condition over a long period of time.

She probably didn't even know what I meant as she was in such denial about her mental illness. It took about eight years before we got back into contact. Though the cut-off was extremely difficult, I still feel it was the right decision for me.

I don't believe you have to give anyone the power to disturb your mind or to harm you. We each have the right to protect ourselves, even against our parents. I'll stand by this to this day.

I realized that it was possible that she could die during this time and feel fortunate she did not. I just had to take that risk. It was time for my needs, and the needs of my children and husband, to take priority.

I considered her an insoluble problem. One solution was that she would die, relieving us all, of the quandary we were in. And though I did not outwardly wish that, I was okay with it. I felt that I had given her my best while living with her. I felt I'd paid her back. She gave birth to me and took care of me and I helped her as much as I could when I lived with her, so to me the score was even.

I recognize that my decision about how to survive was controversial. It goes against our tribal consciousness. What the tribe would say is you stick with them no matter what. They can abuse you and you have to take it. What I was doing was breaking a tribal law. It was a bold thing to do. I don't expect that most people could do this or even understand it. Most people feel you have to do whatever the family wants you to do, even if it's harmful and abusive.

I think my behavior enabled others in the family to set limits on her also, hanging up the phone on her if she was inappropriate. It did undermine her power base, which was a good thing. At first I was judged by some of my siblings. They thought it was harsh, but now they understand it.

Some of this was innate; some was my childhood environment. I had to rely on myself, and make my own way in the world. A large portion of my strength came from studies of psychology and family therapy. It enabled me to understand roles, rules, boundaries, and communication processes so I could better navigate through, and not be trapped by, the dynamics of a family or other system. I was influenced by many of the early pioneers of family therapy such as Satir, Bowen, Minuchin, Whittaker, Haley and others.

From reflecting and processing my dysfunctional relationship with my parents, I came to understand what healthy, secure attachment is and to bring it to the parenting of my own children. I continue to learn and grow, and in the last decade have come to understand relationships even more deeply from my training with Sue Johnson and John and Julie Gottman.

My path is to study relationships, so I can help others transform theirs. I first became a Gottman Certified Couples therapist, then went on to become certified in Emotionally Focused Couples Therapy, developed by Sue Johnson. That model enabled me to fully develop and apply my understanding of attachment to couples relationships and to develop a fully secure attachment with my husband.

Change Catalyst

My master's program was in Psychiatric Mental Health nursing in Chicago. Our first assignment was to go into our community, make an assessment, and figure out how to enter a system and to make changes. It was at the beginning of the community mental health movement and nurses were integrating this approach into their program.

When I finished my masters' program, I worked as a therapist for a couple of years. Then I was teacher and practitioner in a very exciting Bachelor of Science in Nursing program at Rush University, teaching half time, practicing the other half. I had responsibilities on the hospital psychiatric unit and took my training to this unit. I often had to do battle with a "Nurse Ratchet" -type person; a woman with a lot of power. I was encouraged by my boss to face off with her. I was willing to go against a strong system, as I had done in my family.

I was interested in doing things differently and was able to make constructive changes. When young, we definitely have more energy to fight the system and I had been trained to do that. Innately, part of who I am is to be a catalyst for change. I think of myself that way and feel it is my soul's purpose. If you want to be a catalyst, you have to be willing to stick your neck out and do things to make something different happen.

More Changes

Later I knew I needed to leave Chicago. I felt I would never find a partner there. For some reason, it felt to me like a dead-end on the relationship front. I did not see a future there for myself, so I trusted my instincts and moved. I packed up my car with some of my belongings, stored the rest, and set out in search of adventure and a new place to live. I spent two months camping across the US by myself – not something most women have done. I had moved during my Saturn return (astrologically speaking) at age twenty-eight.

I didn't find any place that felt like home until I reached the S.F. Bay area. At first it was very frightening, but eventually I adjusted. I was able do this because I knew how to fend for myself. I'd learned I couldn't count on anyone else to make things happen for me. Shortly after arriving, I got a job in a Community Mental Health Center, where I met my future husband. I went for an interview at an outpatient program and they'd put Peter in charge of making sure I took the job.

I was immediately attracted to him, though he was married at the time, so I went off and found another boyfriend. Nine months later, this relationship broke up as Peter was breaking up with his wife. The timing was perfect and we began dating.

Once I began a relationship with Peter at age twenty-nine, my life started to improve dramatically. My depression lifted, and I remained depression-free until menopause. I finally had a secure attachment figure, so I didn't have that abandonment depression. I felt like someone was there for me.

Women as Mentors

I did have women mentors along the way, and each meant a lot to me. In undergraduate school, my psychiatric nursing instructor took a special interest in me, giving me a sense of support and encouragement. I got a grant from the National Institute of Mental Health to go through graduate school, thanks to Sheila McMahon, who encouraged me in the application process.

After graduate school, my first job had a Ph.D. prepared nurse named Michelle Cunningham, who offered support and validation. She was there during my summer work and also my first job. My supervisor in family therapy training after graduate school, Sandra Watanabe-Hammond, was another woman I looked up to and offered me support. I did find powerful women along the way, which I benefited from and remain grateful for.

What I (Mostly) Love About Aging

What feels good to me now, as I age, is having a lot of wisdom and life experience to share with people, whether my clients, children, or friends. I feel that I actually know something now; when you are in your twenties and thirties, you feel that you should know things, so you can get caught up in more external knowledge (facts and information).

At our age we have gathered bushels of wisdom, and I've learned from all that I've devoted my life to, including my personal and professional growth, raising a family, having a partner, etc. To be honest, however, in my peri-menopausal and menopausal years, my genetics caught up with me. When we are young, we are protected by our resilience. As we age, however, some of our genetics come to the forefront. Traumas also turn on certain genes and cause them to be expressed physically.

I have been learning to deal with and to heal so many aspects of my life. I spent the first forty-five years healing emotionally, mentally, and spiritually. The last fifteen I focused on physically healing myself. This became a big part of my path -- learning to read, know and honor my body, so I could be honest about it, do what is right for it, be honest and embrace it. I discovered I cannot eat much sugar, milk, gluten, caffeine, spices, or alcohol.

It was fascinating to learn about my bodily needs. I learned to honor and abide by them and that resolved many health issues. I have a lot of interest in so many levels of healing. Food as medicine is the path I've been on, healing myself through diet, herbs and "nutraceuticals" (pharmacy-grade vitamin products), also healing myself by detoxification.

I have also learned about what healthy eating is – especially for me. Each person has to refine the basics for themselves, learning what to eat as well as to not put unnecessary toxins into the body.

Awakening our Consciousness

As a therapist, I have had the privilege to participate intimately in the lives of thousands, bypassing all the social chatter and getting down to what is really important. I've learned so much in my forty years of working with people -- from my own successes and failures personally and professionally, to from having the benefit of the collective wisdom of all these people.

Doing this work, I've honed my intuition and my ability to see beneath the surface. Now I have all of that to share. Personal growth work is about becoming more conscious and aware. Living a consciously awakened life is what I've always strived for. At first I worked on the mental/ psychological /emotional levels, then on the body level. The more conscious I've become about my body, the easier it is to make healthy choices.

Gems from Jan

- *Pay attention to the feedback you're getting from life.*

- *Go inside, learn about and explore yourself.* Don't be afraid to know your thoughts, feelings, beliefs, and what is true in your relationships.

- *Hold an open mind to find your truest path.* You may not know it yet, but hold the space for it to come to you.

- *A prayer I say every day comes from astrologer Caroline Casey,* "Open my path before me, allow me to express my gifts, and be of maximum good in the world." It keeps me focused on making good decisions.

- *Cultivate your intuition so you can learn to trust it.*

- *One thing I loved as a child was reading biographies and autobiographies.* I've read hundreds of them. That is why I love my job now. It's fascinating to hear people's stories and my work is to help people re-story their life.

- *If you don't like the story you're stuck in, change it.* You may need help - a mentor, therapist, or group. It is valuable to have people outside yourself to reflect back to you.

- *What has helped me most is to use resources available to me to change and grow, and I've become a resource to help people change and grow.*

- *Never stop learning and growing.* Don't ever feel you have to be stuck; it is all about *intention* and *attention.* Get clear that you want to change and how, then put attention on making steps towards your goal.

- *Chip away at it day by day, Persevere.* That has helped me so much. "The journey of a thousand miles begins with the first step." (Chinese Proverb)

A Tribute to Eleanor Schuster, RN, PhD

Grande Dame Professor of Holistic Nursing

The editor and Eleanor

I first met Eleanor at a holistic nurses conference. She was stunning, with her tall graceful stature, white hair swirled into perfect waves. The dress she wore was velvet, a deep maroon enhanced with pale lace. It seemed to stretch from floor to ceiling. She was one tall drink!

At our very first meeting, Eleanor pulled me aside, showing me her various tattoos. The first was delicate, upon her wrist. She had another on a leg. She spoke of each fondly, as if they were her children. She wanted a fourth, her butterfly, in a rather delicate place, if my memory serves. She had apparently lived quite a full life, based on the few tales that managed to slip from her lips at quiet times.

Eleanor was a force of nature, devoted to protecting our environment. She had created environmental conferences long before it was popular to do so. At Florida Atlantic University (FAU), she boldly presided over a group of Ph.D-prepared nurses in the creation of a nurturing, holistic healing modality. The nurses teaching at FAU performed their work with such obviously clear joy. They knew something in their hearts that made their work holy. I so enjoyed being with each of them. They were like "nursing nuns."

Eleanor was in a class by herself, and proud of it. This university welcomed and honored her; her words were golden, and her colorful, masterful visions were given careful attention and she was given full reign in the direction she took her program. She fully relished her role as matriarch, wearing it with great pride. She was our Nurse Artist in Residence.

At her inspiration, we took a dusty room in the back of one of the engineering buildings, cleaned it, and created a holy space. This was a place, within the university setting, where nurses and nursing students could go during busy and challenging days, a place to breathe, to relax; a place to heal. Eleanor named it "The Kiva."

The Kiva was our place to join with others, learning to meditate. We shared knowledge as women did in ancient times, woman to woman. We learned first to honor our selves, to keep our self holy. We learned the aesthetics of creating healing environments. Eleanor had clearly captured the vision of Florence Nightingale, a warrior healing woman. She understood that we are of the Earth, and we return to the Earth.

She took good care of her body and was vegetarian for decades. She wore folded lacy socks, long flowing skirts and long, dangly earrings well into her seventies. Her elegance was distinctive and inspirational. She did it her way.

Eleanor was a pacifist, a Quaker. She brought us to Quaker meetings, where everyone is welcomed. We sat in silence together. People speak as they are moved to do so, or they sit, together, in silence. She spoke with the authority of someone who has lived a long and challenging life, who knew her own heart, and who was preparing the world to go on without her. It was clear to me, in my three years teaching there, that Eleanor, while also a scientist, was also a true Master in the Art of Nursing.

Today, Eleanor Schuster's spirit is infused into every aspect of the new *Christine E. Lynn College of Nursing* at FAU. Naturally lighted buildings have replaced a crumbling one. Her spirit also is infused into the curriculum, where her visions were honored and her words were gospel. Special appreciation goes to past FAU Nursing Dean, Dr. Anne Boykin, who recognized Eleanor's gifts and allowed them to inspire our program into one that teaches nurses self-care throughout the healing process of others.

Eleanor's death was much like her life. For a while at the College of Nursing, the world stood still. We each took turns caring for her, as she lay dying in her hospital bed. A bladder cancer had traveled throughout her body and palliative care was the only option she would consider. She continued to communicate her wishes with us as she weakened, even as she was no longer taking in fluid. Her spirit was so strong that it took nine days after end of treatment and sustenance, including water, for her to die. She was calm at the end, drifting in and out of consciousness, small groups of nurses gathered around her. She was the queen amongst us.

Eleanor is known for spearheading the crucial movement to bring holism back into nursing in the university setting. She is also known, worldwide, for her passionate care for our environment. Her impact on those who knew her remains profound.

Creators are often unique; making them special to us. We depend upon leaders, like Eleanor, to show us new ways. I applaud the faculty at FAU Nursing for having the vision, courage, and foresight to hire such a remarkable woman who enriched the lives of many. Eleanor's spirit is so woven into the new nursing buildings there; I can easily imagine that today's FAU nursing students hear her singing or drumming even now.

I pay a special tribute to Dr. Eleanor Schuster, who led with a soft voice and an iron will. She got the job done.

I wanted to seal my bond with Eleanor as she was making her crossing. I wanted to honor her as a mighty force in this world, wishing her well, with a proper farewell. The regal yet simple home where Eleanor lived for years in Florida was a reflection of her in so many ways. In that yard, she was known to have enjoyed more than one cigar and Bombay Gin-enhanced evening. Needless to say, it held that same wonderfully healing energy. As she lay peacefully waning, I found myself picking up a bottle of Bombay Gin and a cigar. I drove over to her house at dusk one night, sat in her yard, in that same old lawn chair that she sat in for years and, looking at the night sky, I toasted her. Eleanor was now dancing with the stars.

If we have lived a good life, if we have worked hard to love and be loved, then we shall be missed. Our work is never done; it is ongoing. We can learn to use our gifts, to live moderately, to be good to the Earth. Let us be proud "Students of Life." Let others show us their gifts as we acknowledge their progress, giving them a chance, as we have been given.

Let us increasingly find fun ways to honor those whose work exceeds our expectations and to those that bring us joy, so they know we care.

Let us listen to our lives, laughing at the funny parts, crying when we feel sad. Let us remember to share our burdens.

Let us rejoice in our unique and wonderful gifts, in Eleanor's honor.

Kathleen Shaffer
Working for a Better Community

"Change forces us to see things in new ways."
~ Kathleen Schaffer

We live in a quaint small 7,000 resident town called Sebastopol, an hour north of the Golden Gate Bridge. And Kathleen, our city councilwoman, walked to every home in our community, meeting the people and hearing their concerns. She then brought those

ideas back to city council, where she fought for what she, and our residents, believes is just and fair.

Though Kathleen is someone I met more recently, I find her exceptionally inspiring in many ways. She performs her work with great enthusiasm, as if born for this role. As president of the homeowners association in a senior living park, I invite Kathleen to attend our HOA meetings, providing us a valuable direct link to our city council. She's fought for us and guided us in our process with excellent results and though not all will agree with certain decisions, she is universally respected for her attention and caring. I feel supported and nourished by her willingness to help our citizens, and seniors. I wanted to understand how she got so good at what she does. Here is what she shared:

In the Beginning

I had some bumps early in my life. My mother worked at the nursery I attended. It was a well-known place in Louisville, owned by a wealthy woman who'd never married. She used her money to start a neighborhood house, one of the first of its kind. Mom left in the afternoons, but had me stay for naptime. I remember tossing and turning on my cot, unable to rest as this woman sat in a nearby chair and said mean things to me that the other kids could hear. I never repeated this to my mother. I think I may have been too afraid.

I now understand that for whatever reason, she was upset with my mother, but took it out on me. It truly affected me in many ways. In a crowd of people, even today, I don't like to be singled out. Now, though I am in the public eye, I choose not to be recognized. I like to go to meetings without being called on and prefer to just listen and not be noticed. I like to be public only when I choose to be.

On Change

I've gone through lots of changes and know what it can do to people. I remember moving out to the suburbs, which was a complete 180 from my former life. We had lived in an old house and then we moved to a brand new one. Mother had grown up in this new town and father wanted a fresh start. I don't think that move was happy; in fact, I think mother was miserable. It was a hard time for the family.

The change helped the kids, however. It was more affluent and the kids living there went to college, which was new to me. I went to school in Eastern Kentucky and saw a lot of kids from Appalachia going to school. That was an awakening. Change forces us to see things in new ways.

On Ambition

I feel it is so crucial that we have choices. Women need to have confidence and be able to choose wisely. I learned about ambition, wanting to be successful, even while things were not great for women. Back then you either became a teacher or nurse. The feminist movement in the 70s found me putting all my ambitions into my partner, but my husband wasn't ambitious. Rather than pushing myself, I pushed him.

I helped get him into graduate school, which he was unable to complete. Soon thereafter, the marriage dissolved as I realized I wanted more from life. So I got it my own master's degree in organizational development from University of California, San Francisco. I was ambitious, worked hard and learned so much from the experience.

Community

I am now trying to help the residents in my community to have adequate and affordable resources. But not every decision is an easy one. I don't feel it's a good time to add sales tax, however, after speaking with our finance director, I now know how desperately my city needs revenue -- as do most in the US. We need roads paved, but our finances are in the red. We do have some funds and are trying to fix our town up, as we can. If circumstances become more bleak we will need to talk about it, but I feel we just can't keep raising rates in these trying economic times! We must make all our decisions with great care today.

Family Lessons

My dad wanted us to be successful. He wanted us girls to get two years of college and the boys, four. He had the foresight to know we needed to change the status quo and saw opportunities for us to succeed. A smart man, he taught me to make and take advantage of opportunities. *Find success and go for it.* He also taught us to make goals as a couple, and that trust is essential. My parents, so impacted by the war, were often at odds with each other, and the lack of trust was devastating. He wanted us to learn from their unhappiness.

I'm grateful for those lessons as my husband, Bob, and I work together in our family business. We're not terribly social, so we rely on each other. Bob's parents were farmers in Indiana and they were raised to be very cautious, to be afraid of authority and to never question. They have their routines where they feel safe. But the war changed a lot; we don't have to go through what they did in the Depression. I didn't want to be like that as an adult.

I also had a lot of early experiences that taught me resilience, and helped me learn what I didn't like. Now I make decisions by looking at the situation. I evaluate how a person has treated others and whether he has good or bad intentions. Whether it ends up hurting me or not, I can't support or help someone that I don't think deserves it. I have learned to trust my gut; we all know things this way, but many have not learned to trust it.

Women Who Inspire

I am amazed that even women will select white men for roles that could easily benefit from having a woman in role. After all, Madeline Albright knew what to do, and she did it. And Elizabeth Edwards was a strong courageous woman who pushed her man forward when she could have been a leader herself. Most of us know the sad end of her story.

When I reflect on the life of Eleanor Roosevelt, I wonder, why put yourself through that misery? She even allowed her children to treat her poorly as they grew. I would have raised hell! Just lead on your own, which she could have done. Geraldine Ferraro, who ran for Vice President of our country so long ago, was great, but she was hampered by her husband's business challenges. Georgia O'Keefe was married; she left and did her own thing, and continued to paint. Michelle Obama is strong and powerful. Maybe things are changing.

Making a Difference

One person can make a difference. Women – and men – can make a difference. Having the ideas, energy, and stamina allows even one person to start something. I have always thought that making a contribution to one's community is both gratifying and fulfilling. I have been involved in many organizations, usually of a political nature, and always tried to relate our activities to the community.

I thought running for office would be an interesting endeavor, but the responsibility involved with owning our business made it almost impossible for a while. I always thought about the women I knew who held elective office, and drew comparisons with their strengths and accomplishments to my own and knew if the opportunity ever arose, I would also run for office.

Now that we live in the small city of Sebastopol, where there are so many opportunities and organizations in which to be involved, I thought it would be good to consider running for the City Council. I talked with my husband, as well as our friends and associates to see what they thought. Their support for the idea convinced me to run, and I won.

I have truly enjoyed the work. Being involved in decisions that impact our city, developing strategies that will improve our safety and planning for our growing older population is challenging. It requires a lot of time and making compromises with my husband, but we have agreed to share time with each other's organizations. Each of us can make a difference.

Women have to put themselves out there, as a person, and play to win. If playing with old boys, play their game. We still don't have equal pay, and women are still with the ones most often raising the kids, but we need to persevere. Improve yourself for your community – and for humanity.

On Goals

My goal presently is to get re-elected to our City Council. Even though politics is demanding, even at the local level, I want to create a balanced life; one where my husband doesn't feel shut out. My goal is to strike a balance. I also aim to get a Facebook page for our town, helping to share our good news and concerns. My goals involve continuing to improve both my community and my personal life.

Gems from Kathleen

- *You do have choices.* Always try to keep yourself in a position where you can make choices. Even with children, make sure you are self-reliant, so you can help your children and yourself.

- *Exercise and take care of yourself, so you have long healthy life.* I have the belief that everyone needs to stay as healthy as we can eat well and wisely. I like running; I can go by myself at my own timing.

- *Stay involved* – know what's going on around you.

- *Be aware* – don't get surprised or caught short. Pay attention to all aspects of your life.

- *Stay young and healthy at heart.* Be sure to stay open to changes.

Karilee's note: Kathleen, surprisingly to many, was not reelected to our city council. I trust she will be led to her next calling, where she can share her strong caring skills.

Her leadership and modeling has enriched our town.

Thank you, Kathleen, for blessing us with your gifts.

Lovely Laurina
The Power of Commitment

*"When people don't speak up, they are
relinquishing responsibility for our world,
and therefore are responsible for what is occurring."*
~ Laurina Hildering van Lith

*Next, I would love to introduce you to a very special friend. She
and her husband traveled all the way from Amsterdam to see
my husband and me in our medical practice, because she was
not getting the help she needed for her thyroid care in Holland.
Laurina said that she felt very inspired by our books, where she
said she found deep caring and understanding of the processes
of healing. That gave her hope and made her want to see us.*

In meeting her, we instantly saw so many parallels in our lives, as women, mothers, and healers. She is a psychologist, interested in women's issues and married to a dynamic and visionary physician. It was a perfect fit. Laurina was one of the first psychologists in Holland to major in psychology and psychotherapy of women.

Spending time with Laurina was truly a gift. Now I share her with you. We are so fortunate to know such great women who give so much back to life. While she is a very multifaceted person, I may not be able to capture the depth of her essence in this interview, but I have tried. Here she shares her story, her passion and her love for children.

Speaking with Laurina recently reminded me of the wonderful gifts she models for our world. Despite her ongoing health challenges, which many of us sensitive women face, she speaks with crystal clarity, explaining "It is important that we learn from each other how to live." Together, we can create a better model for women; one that honors who we are, how we operate, and what we need.

I send blessings to dearest sister, Laurina, whose light helps heal our world.

Laurina's Story

I would first like to dedicate this story to my youngest daughter Lili, whose knowledge of loving has taught me how to love myself.

I was born in Amsterdam, yet I have always been traveling. I love to use my maiden name to honor the matriarchal connection. Even our children have both family names. In fact, the Queen of Holland is working to ensure that women can keep their own names, and give their children their names also at birth, allowing women to choose.

I was the oldest daughter, and practically the only granddaughter in our family. This turned out to be a great risk as we shall see later, because the sexual abuse focused upon me. Yet the family also provided role models from which I took strength. My father was in the Dutch Resistance in World War II; this was very influential to me, growing up.

Learning to Stand Up

My matriarchal grandmother's two brothers, resistance fighters, were shot and killed by Germans; other family members, including female members of the family, were in hiding and doing resistance work, as well. I remember very well my grandmother's sadness and saying to myself "I'd rather be an active fighter than a sad person staying behind and feeling passive and tearful always."

At a very young age, I was touched by the tremendous suffering from that war, but also by the fact that we can each make a choice. Those who were brave took a stand; they were very inspiring to me, and as a result, found myself doing that for much of my life.

If I think of what I'm doing now, I am taking a stand. When I was young, I was usually the class representative. If something was unfair, I was the spokesperson. I was timid, very shy and not loud, but injustice made me speak up. I also confronted teachers when things did not feel right. Sometimes I stood alone in this, challenging authority. I clearly remember how frightened and confused it made me feel to be courageous, and to stand up and speak for a good cause, only to have others, who may agree with me, be afraid to speak up and stand by me.

Standing alone used to frighten me, but that was never a reason to not do it. I listened more to the voice inside of me saying I could not live with myself if I don't speak up, so just do it. I felt inspired by my resistance-fighting family members or brave people and thought, "I cannot let them down!"

I feel it makes for a dull life when one doesn't speak one's truth, for then you have no influence. In our daily lives, we all see bad things; I feel that if we don't speak up, we are allowing them to happen; that others are controlling life and not you. To this day I find it sad that people fear speaking up, allowing terrible atrocities to occur.

One example of this is in my city, Amsterdam. For all my life and the lives of my family before me, we traveled everywhere by bicycle. Recently, however, little noisy scooters are exploding in our city, dramatically changing the atmosphere. The number of lethal accidents has skyrocketed. While I know there are many people who condone it, they won't speak up.

This – destroying nature – is happening to Mother Nature and the Earth, as well. I must admit, I am tired of people saying they don't like the government, yet they won't do their part to make the world better. When people don't speak up, they are relinquishing responsibility for our world and therefore are responsible for what is occurring.

Finding Strength

I have never felt helpless or hopeless. I grew up with authoritarian parents, and sadly, as a very young girl, was sexually abused. Then, when I was older, was raped at knifepoint for five hours. I literally had to fight for my life, fight to survive. It has changed my life. I want to reach out to other abused women because really it is undeserved shame that prevents us from sharing these experiences. As women we often feel guilty, when really we are absolutely NOT responsible.

American women have done a wonderful thing when they stopped saying abuse victims but rather say abuse survivors, because that recognizes our strengths. I have always felt very inspired by the frank way American women address women's issues and hope that they will continue to be an inspiration to women worldwide. That frankness is needed, now more than ever, with fundamentalist religions growing in influence.

I have supported my children in taking a stand, always. I repeatedly told them the most beautiful thing you can have is your own values. When my eldest daughter came home with mice that she stole from the biology lab because she didn't want them killed, I supported her against the school principal and kept them in our house.

During the Vietnam War, I was a student leader. At that time, people came from Kent State University to Amsterdam. I loved listening to them and was inspired by the fact that they came to our small country to talk to us; that they reached out to share their opinions. Those of you who are younger may not remember that at Kent State, students were shot and killed by the US government for protesting the war. It was a very turbulent time.

Deepening My Work

I loved participating in the revolts back then. I was most engaged with women's groups, NOW (National Organization for Women) and other women's awareness groups, which eventually led me to study psychology of women. I was one of the first women in Holland to graduate in psychology and psychotherapy for women. We recruited Professor Doris DeHardt, PhD from

California, because there was no one here to teach psychology
of women. I loved her classes and soaked up every word. For
the first time I felt that the university touched upon my own
real life and things that really mattered to me. Even after 30
years, I remember her classes and still find them relevant; in
fact, my youngest daughter is now using one of her textbooks.
Unfortunately, the male professors avoided her and she left early.

During and then after university I added bodywork (Reichian,
Gestalt, and others) to my counseling with women. At that time,
many Americans were coming over and teaching bioenergetics.
I could see the value and interconnections of this work. I studied
in the United States and in Israel, combining energy work with
therapy. As a student, I was asked by several film directors to work
for them. Although I liked the work very much, I did not pursue
this career because I had a few very unpleasant experiences with
movie directors, who pressured me sexually. The only Dutch
role model there was at the time was an actress, who was known
internationally for her role in the soft porn movie, *Emmanuelle*.

Conflict and Resolution

When I came of age in the 1970s, our choices were limited. If
times were different and I had healthy female role models, I
would have perhaps not chosen the career I did. I regret that
I did not see that as an actress, I could have used my fame to
convey a message to the world. I feel if I had known a woman
like Angelina Jolie, I would not have felt a conflict between

wanting to help women in a (proper) traditional women's role as opposed to profiling myself as an actress – but would have combined both!

Influential actresses came later. I did however have the great fortune to work with a very famous director, Theo van Gogh. However, van Gogh was murdered in 2004 because he made a very beautiful, courageous and impressive film, titled *Submission*, about the oppression of women in traditional Islam. He made this film with Ayaan Hirsi Ali, a survivor of a brutal genital mutilation as a young girl in Ethiopia, who had to flee to the US after the film's release as she was no longer safe in Holland. Some parts of Amsterdam are now 50% Islamic, and this controversial film had put her at great risk. She is now in Washington where she works for a Think Tank about Freedom. While I miss her very much, I applaud her efforts and feel that women should be aware.

Looking back, I realize that my traditional upbringing gave me no values for profiling myself; that is why being an actress really felt wrong because as a woman I was taught rather to give, and nurture, put myself last. That is why psychology felt more natural. Theo's brutal murder and Ayaan's flight were both turning points in my life.

Then I married, established a private practice, and am now a mother of three. All my children were born in water, at home. I truly feel that giving birth naturally, in a home environment,

~~is one of the most empowering of all experiences a woman~~ can have. I experience deep sadness when I consider the over-medication that deprives women of this fantastic, life-changing opportunity.

I'm likewise very sad that homebirths and breastfeeding are rapidly declining and that, because of work pressure, young mothers often do not really surrender to the joys of birthing, pregnancy and breastfeeding. This deprives them from feeling nurtured by the love given by their babies and leads them to exhaustion, rather than joy and strength they could find through mothering.

Amsterdam's Welvaren- the Story of My House

As a child I used to love to see the old houses in Amsterdam, especially looking at the gable stones, ancient pictures and the proverbs and conundrums on them. Thirty years ago, my husband and I purchased our home, called *Amsterdam's Welvaren*. Its story begins in 1790, when the American war of Independence was fought. Of course one of the issues between the Americans and the English was the abolishment of slavery. During that war, the Dutch supported the United States against the British, because the Dutch were slave-traders, earning massive fortunes, and thus supported the Americans in their wish to continue slavery.

The British, however, wanted to abolish slavery, largely under influence of the British Quakers. The Quakers were pacifistic, in favor of women and children's rights, very driven by deep values. The British king had given letters of piracy to British captains so that they could capture enemy ships. When a captain of the British ship, called *The Nancy,* spotted Amsterdam's *Welvaren* (meaning well-faring), a Dutch ship returning from the West Indies in the British channel, they were allowed to capture it and loot it. They sailed the ship to Limerick in Ireland. They discovered that there was a huge fortune in gold in the ship. They insured this fortune by Lloyds in London and then wanted to sail it to London.

However, a huge storm sank the ship in the Irish Sea. Lloyds had to pay the British. One of the three owners of *The Nancy* benefited enormously from this payout. His name was John Warder, and he was a Quaker. For forty years, the Quakers reasoned with him that this money was an act of war and therefore against their pacifist principles. Finally he created a fund from all the money he had received from Amsterdam's *Welvaren,* which still exists today.

Now the other Quakers had to find a good purpose for this fund. First they had paid the Dutch captain of Amsterdam's *Welvaren* and gave bread to the poor, but a huge fortune was still left. They found their purpose when a Dutch Quaker visited London who was inspired by the new infant schools (kindergartens) found there.

Quakers were very devoted to supporting the poor and overworked mothers in the city. They decided to build the first kindergarten in Amsterdam with funds from this trust. So they bought a house built in 1636 in Amsterdam, and created a kindergarten with free tuition for poor children. It was a very enlightened and modern school, with excellent teachers and 120 pupils and became the first kindergarten in the Netherlands.

In 1860, they created a beautiful building in Neo Gothic style more suited to serving as a school, and it operated until thirty years ago. Not just a school for young children, this was a mission, and an asset to the neighborhood.

In 1948 the Quakers received the Nobel Prize for peace, because in World War II, they supported victims on both sides of the conflict. In the acceptance speech of the Nobel Prize, Mister Cadbury spoke a long time about our house.

He mentioned that when a person lives according to certain deep values, this is very enriching, but also sometimes very challenging, as is shown by the 40 years it took for the Quakers to solve the situation between the three countries, find a good solution for the money and reason with John Warder to make up his mind. John Warder had moved to the US later in his life. It is not always easy to walk your talk, as a later part of the story of the house shows.

This *Welvaren* kindergarten was the home I purchased decades ago. I was so inspired by this story, which has become a thread through my life, for it came about through people standing up for the right thing and together people came to a good solution. I knew it wasn't just a normal house, but a special space. While we lived there, we would reserve a large part of the house for groups, meditation, satsangs, or other good purposes. This was all part of my commitment to the mission statement written by the founders, on the wall. They felt that this house should do good work in the neighborhood, since times are not always easy for families.

Darkness

A dark period started in 1997. I took a sabbatical in the States, wanting to specialize in working with abused children. We had to have someone move into our house for the year we were gone, to protect it. We felt we had chosen well, but shockingly, the caretaker destroyed the historical elements, damaged the sound structure, ruined the original style, and then did not pay the rent, refusing to even move out. He caused massive damage, both physically to the house and mentally to me and to my family. In Holland there are very strong protections for renters and even though he broke the contracts he signed, I knew it would be very hard to evict him.

Standing absolutely stunned, in the formerly beautiful, simple and elegant Shaker-style classroom, now unrecognizable,

I knew this would be a tough fight. I told him that the house was entrusted to me and that I would get it back and restore it, that I would fight for it with all that it took. Here, everything I learned in life and all my values truly came to the test, just like my ancestors in the war.

We all experience moments of true choice. I was only the second owner in all these hundreds of years. How could I let it be destroyed? I considered the mission statement, "Now may it long remain and be unto the neighborhood as the name of the captured ship indicates, Amsterdam's *Welvaren.*" So it was written on the beautiful triptych on my walls, and so it should remain, and do good. It was not about my private gain; instead, I saw this as my trust, my contribution to my neighborhood and community. I must protect it. It was truly a cultural treasure.

Returning from U.S., we moved into the basement of our house. There was no light. We had to share one room with our three children. Moreover, the air was bad because he had also destroyed the air conditioning. Living there was the only way to prevent further damage and to watch him. It took two years to win the court case and all told, we lived in that basement for over three years. I got to know him very well living underneath him. It took me a long time to understand why he had to damage this sweet and innocent looking schoolhouse for small children. It turned out that he abused young children and could not tolerate the innocent style.

The whole process was also my own healing. I was working in therapy dealing with my own abuse as a girl, reclaiming my authority over body and self. I learned a lot about the deep-seated mechanisms of abuse in our society. I was fighting for my house and reclaiming it from the abuser upstairs as well. It was tough, but being in a small space also brought us very close as a family. Because we felt so strongly about it, we felt clear about our purpose. I had given up my job and worked exclusively on winning the court case.

In the end, miraculously, the judges came to the house. I had been praying for a wise judge, just like in the bible story of Solomon with the two mothers. The judges had refused our tenant's higher appeal, and while visiting the house and seeing the damage, they looked at the tenant and suggested he leave. After that, they looked at me and suggested I withdraw my demands for the half a million euro in damages. The judge explained this was to end the case quickly, by a covenant. I looked in the judge's eyes and realized he was telling me to take this offer, even though it hurt so much financially, and we had absolutely no money. I knew that this was wisdom.

It did not feel good, yet I knew I had to accept, trust that the money would be found to restore the house, and sign the covenant. It would finally be over for the kids. Unfortunately, when the tenant moved out he caused even more damage. Strangely enough, he was a very well known person and even visited the royal family and drew the Queen's portrait. Living in one house with him and observing his abusive nature from so close, I got too know him very well, including the sides of him that were well hidden from the public and the Queen. I knew a great many scandalous things about him that I could have brought out to the press but did not.

Throughout my ordeal, I felt the integrity of the Quaker founders speaking to me and I didn't want to let them down. I feel that the modern press, thriving on so much scandal, can cause a lot of harm. It was a great privilege to be in this situation and learn about choosing the right thing, the wisdom that comes from that.

It took all we had to restore the house. Our family had to relocate for a year while it was being restored. The court case was so difficult that I ended up with burn-out, low thyroid, and menopause all at the same time. My house was so violated, and I came to realize it was a representation of my early life, where I had been violated in a dark basement. In our society there is almost no protection for the young and innocent.

Moving Ahead

I came to see this battle as a way to heal myself, for it was a parallel story. At first I didn't understand, but halfway through in a meditation and prayer, I discovered my true reason for going through this struggle. I wanted the house to be a Child Empowerment Centre in the future.

Bringing that about would provide great healing and would reconnect the place with its original mission.

So I asked myself: what would the house want? What are the central elements in its story? I came up with three things:

- It is about innovative work with children.

- It is about universal values.

- It is about communication for peace.

The Quakers of course were always about universal values, what all good people share alike. The whole history of the house was about bringing peace between countries, to make up for acts of war. And I must say that I was so supported by wonderful women healers in this process. Their contributions were a heartfelt gift, as were those wise judges. It helped keep me going to receive that level of inspiration.

My Work

The reason for opening up a private practice was that it became increasingly difficult to offer innovative skills within traditional institutions, as they were becoming over-managed, with too many meetings, and not enough progress or change. This was too time-consuming for a young mother.

I have always had my own practice, working with children or adults, sometimes in groups. That is what I do today. Still just working and mothering never felt like my true cause. I have often wondered why I always chose from my heart to prefer giving most of my energy to my children, yet that never really felt like my mission, my voice. That came later, in connecting to the mission of my house, my children's center.

Ten years ago I heard about empowerment work, also from the United States. I studied with motivational speakers who inspired me. This was not from the "medical sickness model" but instead was from helping people to operate from the core power within. I began combining empowerment work with therapy and found that people made progress many times faster with this combination. But there is no failure, for failure leads to learning, learning leads to knowledge, and knowledge leads to power.

I lived in Israel for almost three years. When I was living there, we would often meet with Palestinians and try to find common ground. I believe that wherever we find ourselves, there is work for us there to do.

My advice: *Go out and do what you feel inspired to do.*

If you are motivated to make a difference, stay with it. The most important aspect in change is **decision**. Like Erin Brockovich, any woman can decide to make a difference, if you stick with it. Hearing which voice inside you is most important is critical. Many women are challenged by the combination of work and children. And indeed, wanting to be a good mother, wife and therapist was really hard on me.

I absolutely feel that it is time again for women to come together; to be supportive, and inspiring, combining our different roles to avoid fatigue and burn out. We need to really nurture ourselves and each other. I often worry about young children growing up without enough nurturing, because mothers need to work too much. I feel that supporting young mothers is vital to a healthy society! I find it very sad that nowadays so much emphasis is put on just material wealth. Even sadder is the high divorce rate, leaving mothers and babies poor and struggling.

It's okay to make decisions that allow you to sequence your goals. Allow yourself a whole long life. Don't create pressure that it has to all be done at once. For me, the children were top priority when young. Now that they are bigger, I have more time to devote to larger issues.

I am so grateful to Karilee for creating a platform for women to find their voice. Looking back, I know that that is what was most missing for me. I would just work and work and only give and give, feed, nurture, listen, and make sure to get it all done. There was no time for my own voice and I regret that. Sharing with you is such a gift. I'm sure this is true for most women.

Finding My Cause

Finding my voice came for me with the story of my house and is so symbolic. In defending and reclaiming my house, I rediscovered my true goal and mission in life. Ultimately, this is about defending children. There is enough knowledge on earth now about empowering children and teaching them how to reach their goals and create abundance. I feel that when we reach out and teach a critical mass of children the principles of empowerment, they will inspire others, and our world.

Children can then stay in touch with their unlimited power and potential, and can learn to say "no" to abuse. This really is my biggest dream: child empowerment leading to massive changes in consciousness, resulting in less abuse. There have been societies in history where abuse of women and children did not happen. One of these places was Tibet, which was *polyandric*, meaning one woman could marry several men. Surprisingly, in this culture, jealousy and abuse were not known. Sadly now this is all eradicated by the Chinese invasion, putting an end to this miraculously peaceful society.

As I said, I found my inspiration in the story of my house. Its history has so many elements that I love. It is about choice, commitment, overcoming challenges, making peace between countries, and ends in a Nobel Peace Prize. It is about slavery, America, England and Holland, about womens' rights, looting and pirates. Eventually, all is well that ends well.

During that time, my dear director friend, Theo van Gogh, with whom I worked as an actress, was brutally slaughtered in the streets of my city. It was a fanatically religious-political murder, because he was speaking truth in his films. I prayed, and meditated for some meaning and good to come of this terrible experience. I felt that the mission of the house to bring peace between people was needed even more now. The message of the house would be peace between people, safety for women and children.

Inspired by the history of my house, my friend's murder, my illness and my epiphany, I wanted to now combine these aspects to do my part to contribute. I wanted to help groups now opposing each other to better understand each other. I created a foundation "Bewaar School Amsterdams Welvaren. ('Bewaar' also means to keep safe.) I knew I had to create a systematic plan to make this happen. These were my steps:

1. Get the house back

2. Restore it

3. Provide workshops, initiatives, lectures on empowerment

4. Secure the future of Amsterdam's Welvaren

5. Develop a game to teach children about empowerment.

The first four have now been achieved – and the house is now safe in a trust as a place to be used for growth and healing.

My Advice to Younger Women

Today there is so much available to help you heal and reach your goals. We have the Internet, seminars, books, libraries, and so many different ways to support us to each attain our goals. It's all out there; you must simply trust that your voice and inspiration matter. If you feel inspired and know what you are inspired to do, miracles begin to happen. Look for and allow those miracles in your life.

For example, even as a small abused child, I was not allowed to play outside, but I could read books at the library. I was always guided to the answer I needed. Sometimes I would have a question, and the book would just fall open at the page with the answer. I was so fascinated by that, and it happened over and over. If you want to feel miracles, go for what you believe in, and allow the miracles to happen.

Knowing that each life has value and purpose, your goals can be related to anything that touches you. My dreams for my great, great grandchildren will be that they know they come from an understanding of abundance. We don't have to rule over others, nor abuse the earth, nor cheat, nor steal. Abundance is inside of you. My dream would be that you come to know that the earth deserves responsible stewardship. Realize your greatest challenges will bring the richest rewards. Empower yourself to find exactly what you need, in order to go on and succeed in your dreams. Do your part, no matter how small, for what you feel needs to be done.

I didn't realize when I was fighting for my house that it was a reflection of my earlier life experience as a sexually abused child. Now I know that this fight was actually part of my healing. As I reclaimed my home, as I kicked out the man who reviled it, I was not only doing a community service, I was healing myself. I was helping to restore sanctuary to women the world over by doing my small piece.

I feel our essential nature as women is spiritual. In spirit we are truly strong. In loving, nurturing and protecting, we find our strengths. Nurture yourselves as well. There is a wonderful book, *The Tao of Women*, which speaks of the times that Chinese women were not allowed to study and read. The women secretly taught each other to read by sewing letters in the linens of their hope chests. One of the proverbs was that the wise woman, when she serves, learns to serve herself first. I took a long time to learn that lesson.

Now

We cannot remain stuck in the material realm if we are to change the world and teach our children their true unlimited potential. We must reconnect to loving and nurturing ourselves, and our children. Then everything becomes more fulfilling. Careers are very stimulating, and more fulfilling if there is spiritual growth, as well.

Now having finished the center, I intend to use the knowledge of empowerment, inspiration, and universal values to inspire children all over the world. My goal will be to reach out further into the world, that all children can be safe, free, and united; and come from abundance and peace.

Women must connect more with other women, especially when the children are young. Separation is painful. When we join forces, we inspire each other to remember our true nature. Living so separately keeps us feeling empty. Together our cups overflow. By nurturing each other, speaking our truth; we nurture our world.

Rama Vernon
World Ambassador for Peace

"The Russians were not the enemy; fear was."
~ Rama Vernon

*Allow me to now introduce another beautiful Real Hot Mama,
the last in this book, whom I met years ago through a mutual
friend. Rama not only captured my imagination, she also en-
thralled my two daughters, who loved experiencing her strength
and her commitment. Rama, my daughters and I blended like*

family. We recognized kindred spirits in one another, learning about each other and more about ourselves from being together.

Knowing Rama is a gift I am happy to share, for she shares her love with the world in amazingly beautiful ways. We honor this magnificent woman who has influenced history with her own commitment to inner peace. Traveling to the Soviet Union fifty-three times during the Cold War, she worked in Afghanistan to bring cultures together.

Rama has made the kind of global difference that only a heart full of love can offer. As founder of the Center for International Dialogue, Rama has traveled to organize counterpart meetings, exchange programs, events and conferences. She initiated the First and Second Soviet-American Citizens Summits as well as the first Conflict Resolution and Dialogue Roundtables between Armenia and Azerbaijan, Georgia and the Ukraine. During the Gulf War, Rama formed weekly Arab-American and Middle East Dialogues with citizens of the warring countries.

For the past 20 years, she facilitated women's gatherings throughout the United States. In 1994, she organized the Women of Vision: Leadership for a New World Conference in Washington, D.C., attended by over 500 women. This conference led to the formation of the Women of Vision and Action Network, an international organization that embraces and supports spiritually motivated social action.

On her journey, through the hills and valleys of her work, one thing that kept her going was a quote she found from Eleanor Roosevelt: "If our desire is to serve humanity, we will be crushed and broken hearted. If our desire is to serve God, no amount of ingratitude can keep us from serving our fellow human beings."

I honor the work and spirit of this beautiful and courageous woman!

Rama Vernon: Early Life

I was born into a family of holistic healers. My father was a chiropractor in the early days of that profession; he was also a doctor of naturopathy. My mother was a physical therapist, medical clairvoyant, and one of the first reflexologists in the nation. I grew up earning allowances by giving reflexology to my parents (working on feet to help the entire body feel better).

My parents had a school of naturopathy in our home, so I got my first naturopathy degree at age twelve. I never received vaccinations. I studied with healers from all belief systems, including some who were Christian Scientists.

My father was from Lebanon. He spoke Aramaic (his mother tongue). He never was a fanatic about his religion, but instead he appreciated them all. He was invited to speak in a variety of churches on the original translation of the Bible. He was more like a minister than a doctor.

We worked with many special healers, like Dr. Bates, who helped people naturally correct their eyes. Edgar Cayce followers, Norman Vincent Peale and others came through and studied with him, including Sister Kenney, who did pioneering work with those paralyzed by polio.

He was a true pioneer, and through him chiropractors eventually got licensed in the state of California. He received death threats and was put in jail for practicing without a license, then treated the jailers, and he got licensure for chiropractors with a group of them working together.

I've witnessed many miracles of healing and I believe in everyday miracles, as I've seen so many.

I realized when I was young, growing up in Hollywood, California, that people could become very stuck in their lives. I would see people hanging on to the past, not being able to gear shift into the next era of their life. Very young, at age six, I said I'd rather be a "never was" than a "has been." I wanted to stay in the core of myself so I can make shifts, whether aging, changing jobs, I wanted to be able to make changes as needed. My intention was to always remain true to who I was, not to get lost in what I was doing.

Yoga Years

My mother studied yoga, introducing me into the field. It has since become my life's work. I started the *Yoga Journal*, still popular today. Many others worked with me to bring this into form. Originally published in 1970, over forty years ago, and is available in many languages and a readership of 1.5 million.

I worked to form the California Yoga Teachers Association, teaching teachers of Yoga at a time before others were doing this. In my search, I studied in India, eventually bringing the renown BKS Iyengar to California. This enabled yoga teachers to further their education, which then evolved into Iyengar's Teachers training on the West Coast.

In 1983, I began to form an organization eventually called Unity in Yoga, bringing yoga teachers and students from different yoga paths together. I felt yoga philosophy was universal. It is the basis for all religions, yet not dogmatic. After a while, I began to see that even people in yoga could be dogmatic, believing that only one way is right.

The Dalai Lama once said we are all on the same path. Just because someone follows a different aspect of that path does not mean they are wrong. My motto in those days was, "Truth is one; many are the ways." I worked toward Unity in Yoga, to eliminate competition, and to create non-sectarian yoga conferences. This eventually morphed into the Yoga Alliance, allowing a wide variety of yoga teachers to become certified.

To Russia with Love

I was then called to the Soviet Union. My work had been to help people find inner peace, but I never dreamt I'd be involved in "outer peace." I had always believed that finding inner peace, and radiating it outward, was the way to create world peace. I wanted to eliminate my own inner turbulence, believing that if each does our own work, then that is our gift to the world.

In 1984, I felt called to travel behind the Iron Curtain of the Soviet Union, to see the "enemy" for myself. I stood in Red Square facing fears I had never felt before. I had previously experienced "them" (Soviets) as "the enemy." The first day I stood in Red Square, I felt fear. Then I saw the fear and realized that what we fear is what we draw to us. If we reached a critical mass, with enough Americans fearing Soviets as the enemy, we could create a nuclear war, perpetuated by the governments of the two super-powers.

At that time, fear in the US was pervasive. My children felt they were going to die in a nuclear holocaust. I began to see that this fear conditions minds, thus creating circumstances for governments to control their people. Around this experience, I had a revelation – almost a command from the heavens – to bring thousands of Americans to the USSR, so they could see "the enemy" for themselves, realizing as I had, that the Russians were not an enemy. Fear was. They were just like us.

After returning to the US, I was given an airline ticket in order to meet with a Soviet leader, to whom I would present a proposal to bring Americans to Russia to experience the people as I had, and overcome this cultural fear. At that time, Americans were not allowed to mingle with foreigners, and this protocol was mandatory. Fortunately for me, and the world, the Soviet leader loved my idea. It appeared we had both wanted to find common ground, rather than divisions, since we looked alike as people. He felt my proposal for counterpart meetings to facilitate true dialogue was just what they were waiting for.

I started traveling to Moscow twice a month to meet with officials. Then I was asked to speak in the US, as well as the USSR, about the work I was initiating. It took a year to organize our first group with 85 people. That is when I formed the *Center for Soviet American Dialogue.*

Over the years, we took celebrities, doctors, educators, environmentalists, economists and people from all different walks of life. A venture capitalist from the US wanted us to match him with his counterpart, so we matched him with the only entrepreneur, a black marketer. Dr. Patch Adams joined us; he wanted to bring his gorilla suit and run around in Red Square (those who know Patch will understand). I had to negotiate for that. They said no, so instead he brought red noses. He wanted to bring humor to the situation.

I always believed that the greatest gift I could give to the world was my own inner peace. However, life was now calling me out to do work in the outer world. Over a period of eight years, 53 trips, I took a few hundred groups, with thousands of people, to interact with their Soviet counterparts. Gorbachov said it was groups like ours that helped end the cold war, not just the leaders. It was a great testimony that the individual can make a difference. I also realized that there was no separation between inner and outer peace.

It wasn't easy; there were many sacrifices and changes to do this work. I went through two marriages and had a baby, with incredible transformation during those years; it was the greatest yoga practice I've ever done. I prayed for divine guidance -- with every step I took.

Even As My Knees Shook

The Soviets considered me a brave woman, as I sat with my 3-month old baby on my lap. I did not feel brave; I would quiver with fear. In their culture, bravery means they have courage to face their fears.

It was challenging, but we made amazing inroads into every arena of Soviet society. Barbara Marx Hubbard worked with me to bring top Soviet officials to meet with Americans on the economy, ecology, environment, human rights and religion. Eventually, we were able to establish the first Soviet-American human rights council, as well as almost a thousand joint projects between the citizens of our two countries.

It took seven years to gain their trust, so that we could put on a yoga conference, co-hosted with their Ministry of Health. We even brought one of the yoga teachers jailed in Leningrad for his work in yoga to Moscow, to be a keynote speaker for our yoga conference. The work was powerful, affecting lives on so many different levels. I had no idea what an impact our work would have for the years to come. One of the Soviet officials said, "This work will go far beyond our lifetimes."

I honestly didn't know I could do this. It was one of those urges that arise from a causal level. I was given a vision. I was standing in Red Square in Moscow, living with the threat of nuclear war. I felt in my heart that if I could just stay there, we would not have a nuclear war. I thought it was my ego, but it became real. In 1989, my organization was able to bring KGB members together with former CIA operatives to explore causes of and solutions to international terrorism. Through those years, we even worked with cosmonauts, and astronauts. I was even invited by a group of the cosmonauts to go with them on a future voyage to outer space! I was very tempted.

I must tell you I felt I was guided every step of the way. It required utmost faith, as any missteps could cause great problems. I prayed every minute for guidance, and many times was not sure if I was doing any good. It wasn't for personal profit; I wasn't even getting paid. I had no financial support, and eventually ended up having to sell my house, and give up being with my children, all to do this work.

That 3-month old baby I held in my arms on my trips to Russia, I named "Mira" meaning "peace" in Russian. Now she is studying Aryuvedic medicine, an ancient world form of healing, and is an amazingly peaceful person.

I feel that we as women are so powerful in our 40s and 50s. I want young women to know that sometimes we don't get going until our middle or later years! I started this work at 44 years old, continuing to work into my 60s, 70s and beyond. As I reached these ages, I seem to have more clarity of mind. I feel that if we don't interfere with our body process at menopause, our mind becomes even more clear and focused. Barbara Marx Hubbard says during these years, we move from procreation to co-creation, and I agree.

Afghanistan

Several years ago I was invited to Afghanistan. I had been in other war zones, such as Kosovo, during NATO bombings, as well as in the Middle East. I also had been in Africa, China, and Cuba during non-war times. When I went to Afghanistan, it was a year after the US bombed and invaded on the pretext of hunting *al-Qaeda*. It was surprising to see that Afghanistan is one of the poorest nations in the world; it even makes India look wealthy. Children there learned by writing in the dust with a stick. The people have so little, yet so much heart. I marveled at their adaptability and flexibility, as I worked with orphans, widows and refugees.

We traveled out of Kabul through very primitive land, where women in rural areas still gave birth in stables and traveled hours to the Bhayam Valley, where the huge Buddhist statues had been recently bombed by the Taliban. It was like traveling back 2000 years in time. Huge ancient multi-tiered, hand-carved caves gave me the feeling that dinosaurs could appear at any moment. Incredible dust was all around as we traveled through very narrow valleys. They hauled water from the stream, and carried sticks for firewood on their backs and on donkeys. There was no electricity, no running water; it was a life of simplicity and self-sustaining ability.

I could see young children helping elders, many with only one leg or arm, lost in landmine explosions planted by Russians or US military. Even our driver had lost his leg from the knee down. My heart is so sad; we have created so much suffering in the world. A Russian doctor and I were sitting at the airport in Moscow; he wanted to go with me from Moscow to Afghanistan. He explained, "I was one who was shooting people, now I wish I could go back and heal them."

I worked with the women, teaching yoga to them in their burquas. They threw off their scarves and underneath they wore tight velvet pants with gold cords and tight sweaters. They were wiggling and moving their hips as if they'd been let out of cages! They were beautiful, powerful women, blue silk streaming behind them as they walked majestically down the streets.

One journalist I met in Kabul wore a scarf but not a burqua.

As people were talking about all the destruction, she said very directly, "Men destroy, women rebuild." Women have always had power, now we have simply to realize it, to remember what is true for us. As we speak our truth, we become stronger, demonstrating our value in the service of a greater good.

A New and Challenging Era

My world has changed in recent years. When husband had a stroke, I began working very hard to build a nest egg, realizing that my income would need to sustain us. I was investing in real estate, then noticed the changing patterns in the economy, but did not act, and then the market crashed. I blamed myself and felt guilt. I had never known that feeling. I spent a year feeling shattered, trying to refinance, but nothing was working. I did not realize how bad it would get for the national as well as the global economy.

One time I was so distraught, I did not get dressed for two days. It was my first time ever to feel like I had failed. I was so upset I couldn't meditate; it was a spiritual paralysis. It wasn't about money; it was that I wouldn't be able to have credit. Then I realized I was only losing credit, not my credibility!

I began to see that I was letting the system dictate who I was. I had been making good money, buying, fixing and reselling properties. Then the market crashed, and I got caught in it. My husband and I lost my all my properties and investments. I had to speak with investors, feeling ashamed and guilty.

Shattered, Yet Surprisingly Whole

Amazingly, when I lost it all, I was shattered. My dreams for retirement fell apart. My husband had to go back to ministry. I had to go back to teaching -- and the world is better for it. Because I lost it all, I have returned to the essence of my work, to the fulfillment of my life's destiny.

My goal is to leave a legacy for the yoga teachers, so the work can continue beyond my lifetime. Mature women should not become discouraged when younger people are hired instead of us for jobs. You must keep asking, put yourself out emotionally and spiritually. Ask the universe to guide you so you will know how you can help to ease the pain of humanity, and how you can best serve.

Find stability within yourself so that you can inspire others. Meditation, yoga, self-observation, stress reduction – if we've lost our center, remember how to come back to it. Many people seem lost in their work; when things changed, they couldn't keep up. They often get crushed under sadness, sorrow, or longing for what was. When I was asked to teach yoga, and it grew and grew, I kept thinking I would one day go back to being a housewife and mother. But it hasn't ended yet!

I found other ways to do humanitarian projects. I gave myself time to work on "outer world peace" but eight years later I had several offices and still the work was demanding. I realized there was no difference between inner and outer peace. It was all peace.

Another obstacle I overcame was when I presented Gorbachov with a gift, I saw him surrounded with light. His own people didn't see him that way, but I cried for days after meeting him, I felt that we had been connected in such a deep and indescribable way. We were working in different ways, but when our hands touched, it was one.

On one of my 53 trips to the Soviet Union years ago, I returned home and the roof was leaking. Things weren't being done as I would have liked. I got very angry at my husband. He looked at me sadly and said, "why can't you treat me like you treat the Russians?" His words went through my heart like a spear. It was that moment I realized, "who was I to go out and do peace work and not treat all people in my life with the same respect I would give to Gorbachov and other world leaders?" I made it my commitment not to have separation, nor favorites.

It was a huge obstacle for me to not be critical of others, or not to feel ostracized when criticized by others. I came to believe that criticism could hold people back from claiming their life destinies. People want approval; in seeking it, they may stop due to criticism. I was receiving lots of criticism, but found ways to keep going.

We are criticized at times, but can we learn to stay balanced in the midst of it all? I found it was crucial to find balance between criticism and blame – and compliment and praise. And just keep doing the work, as we feel guided to do.

It reminds me of a time when I gave a talk on my work with US and Soviet relations. Afterward, a woman came up and said, "It's wonderful work that you are doing. Tell me, who authorized you to do this work?" I was stunned. It never occurred to me that I would need to be authorized to do the work I had felt was needed. If I see a need, I just do it. After regaining my composure, I quietly responded to the woman who asked the question, "I authorized myself."

Gems from Rama

My advice to all women trying to create a better world is:

- *Don't be hijacked by the opinions of others* – and don't share the vision before it is ready. Others can't always see what we see. They may come in and destroy your vision. People project their fears when others step out of line. When one does step out, it threatens others who are fearful and afraid to be fully their own true self.

- *Fear is one of the greatest obstacles of all.* I had many medals and honors bestowed upon me. The Soviets kept calling me a brave woman. I kept telling them I didn't deserve that. I told them I was not brave; my knees trembled with fear when I first began the work. I was afraid that someone would get hurt in the process. If anyone ever got arrested due to talking with me, I felt I wouldn't be able to continue the work.

- *I learned that bravery does not mean you are without fear.* It means you have the courage to face your fears. This corresponded to our teachings in yoga. Once a position becomes comfortable, you move into another variation, which represents the unknown. With practice, that new field of the unknown eventually becomes known. In yoga, as in life, we keep moving from the known to an unknown. In that way, we expand the parameters of our life.

- As we get older, we can expand the comfort zones of our life rather than narrow it to a small zone. *We have less and less to lose as we age.* When people close-in their lives due to fears of moving ahead and because of aging, I see this as a great loss to all humanity. The collective consciousness of aging tells us that if you're getting older, you need to start slowing down. We allow the attitudes of others to curtail us, even the belief in the collective psyche that we need to slow down and die. Children can put this on their parents; one needs to remember we have value for all of our days.

- What's quite wonderful is that *experience gives wisdom and insight*. We start to see the patterns rather than the people (the opposite of when we're young). Ego can get easily upset when we're young. What's so important at one time of life becomes so insignificant at another time of life.

- *Aging frees us.* We have less to fear and less fear. If a woman has prepared herself internally, she will have less fear.

- *It is never too late to prepare internally,* and so I continue to help women explore the unknown through yoga. The way we do the pose affects our lives. Movement changes who we are, and who we are becoming, minute by minute.

- *Women have had fear of speaking out,* that we will be "killed." Are we tapping into burning times, when women were killed for doing healing work? Surely, we have a long history of outspoken women being threatened. Yet women continue, finding our ways to share our wisdom. I walk with them. I take their hand, helping them to step across the threshold of their life, so they can move forward. You can be trembling with fear, but facing it will change you. Then you can face other fears that have held you back from your true purpose in life; and you can inspire other women to face their fears.

- Whatever is happening in your life right now, allow it to be. Instead of resisting, *surrender*, go with the flow, allow life to carry you on its waves, and you will enjoy yourself more than you could have imagined.

- *Faith in something greater than ourselves carries us through all storms.* We do not have to do it all, we do have to surrender to our Higher Power, to retain our sense of inner peace and inner joy.

- Learning to love whatever life brings – at any age – is a key component of happiness and fulfillment.

In Closing

A few years ago, I was with the Dalai Lama as he conducted a sunrise meditation on a mountain overlooking the four corners of the Middle East. He stood on the mountainous precipice, with only the early morning sky for a backdrop.

As he turned from side to side his gaze swept over the convergence where, Jordan, Egypt, Israel and Saudi Arabia meet. "I don't see any environmental or natural borders here," he laughed quietly. "Which makes me think that the only borders are within the human mind." That has become an abiding thought for me.

The only borders that keep humanity apart are the borders within the human mind.

Epilogue
Loving the Life You Live

I bless these wonderful wise women, willing to share their stories, dreams and secrets with us. Listening to our "Mamas" can save us a whole lot of time & energy!

To encapsulate their wisdom, here are ideas many contributors shared:

> ➤ Our lives are a long healing journey, a process of restoring ourselves, piece-by-piece, becoming as fully human, and whole, as we possibly can.

> ➤ We tend to choose our path, based upon our past. We can choose more wisely now, each of us learning to enhance our own innate powers of insight, instinct, and intuition. We must be fully present, and learn to speak out to promote healthy change around us.

➢ Listening to my body and my heart, I find my own best ways to heal my life and world. It can also help to reflect with those we love, whose opinions we deeply trust.

➢ You have, within your own self, the keys to heal your life.

➢ Healing is a process, not a permanent state. It is a journey of reclaiming all your parts, of making yourself whole again. Life is a journey of restoration, as we learn to restore our selves to wholeness.

➢ No matter what happened to you, you - & only you - can make yourself, whole.

➢ You are not what happened to you. You are whom you choose to be. You have the potential within you to evolve into your highest vision.

➢ <u>Here is a huge secret</u>: Reclaiming your fullest Self is your gift to our world.

➢ Enjoy your magnificent healing journey. Go ahead inspire us all!

Healing happens – if we will just let it. Dreams are given to us so we can transform our world with our vision and love. Let us continue weaving our stories, to keep us whole and warm. May our growing tidal wave of great outspoken women help to turn things around! Let us, as women, inspire each other to even greater heights. The Earth, herself, begs us to restore balance now.

Remember, **be thankful for the many blessings of your life**. Love what you have been given and bless it. Be grateful for all you have. Learn to see humor in it, and laugh whenever possible!

Honor each person that helps you to grow. Help her at another time or help someone else in her honor. Trust in cycles of Nature, knowing the sun will shine again on your life and world.

Let's do this, Women!

Let us create a tidal wave by sharing great women around us, everyday women who inspire us.

Share the women you love, who inspire you, enjoy every day, & contribute - each in her way.

The conversation continues at:
http://www.AmazingMentorsBook.com
Please join us!